New lifestyles in old age

Health, identity and well-being in Berryhill Retirement Village

Miriam Bernard, Bernadette Bartlam, Simon Biggs and Julius Sim

First published in Great Britain in June 2004 by

The Policy Press
University of Bristol
Fourth Floor, Beacon House
Queen's Road
Bristol BS8 1QU
UK

Tel no +44 (0)117 331 4054
Fax no +44 (0)117 331 4093
E-mail tpp-info@bristol.ac.uk
www.policypress.org.uk

ISBN 1 86134 620 4

British Library Cataloguing in Publication Data
A catalogue record for this report is available from the British Library.

Library of Congress Cataloging-in-Publication Data
A catalog record for this report has been requested.

Miriam Bernard is Professor of Social Gerontology, **Bernadette Bartlam** is a former Research Fellow, **Simon Biggs** is Professor of Social Gerontology and **Julius Sim** is Professor and Head of the School of Health and Rehabilitation, all at Keele University.

Cover design by Qube Design Associates, Bristol
Front cover and photogrpahs used throughout the report © Stephen W. Ellis
Printed in Great Britain by Henry Ling Ltd, Dorchester

Contents

List of tables and figures

Tables

Figures

Acknowledgements

We should like to begin by thanking in particular the residents of Berryhill Retirement Village, many of whom gave up time to complete questionnaires, to take part in the conferencing and discussion groups, and to offer advice and support wherever they could. Our thanks also go to the various family members and friends who helped by completing questionnaires. Everyone made us welcome and we very much appreciated their support over the three years – as well as the cups of tea!

We are also grateful to the local health and social care professionals who took time out from their busy work schedules to be interviewed. Within the local area various individuals, residents and other professionals also gave of their time and energy in supporting the research, and we would like to extend our thanks to them all.

We should also like to thank the staff of the village, who gave up time to be interviewed, to complete questionnaires and to help us organise the various research events in the village. Our special thanks go to Kim Lavelle, Chris Sumner and Vivien Ball for their patient support.

The senior management team at The ExtraCare Charitable Trust, together with Touchstone Housing, took the ultimate risk of allowing external researchers into their 'flagship', and we greatly appreciate their support and help.

The research team was greatly helped by the advice and guidance offered by our Advisory Group who were: Judith Bell (Director of Public Health, Staffordshire Moorlands Primary Care Trust), Angela Bradford (Director of Nursing and Villages, The ExtraCare Charitable Trust), Derek Chawner (resident, Berryhill Retirement Village), Joyce Clewlow (resident, Berryhill Retirement Village), Jan Dutton (Head of Social Work – Adults, Stoke Social Services Department), Stewart Fergusson (Director of Housing Services, Touchstone Housing Association), Peter Hammersley (Chief Executive North Stoke Primary Care Trust), Kim Lavelle, Dr Sheila Peace (The Open University, School of Health & Social Welfare), Liz Taylor (Director, The ExtraCare Charitable Trust) and Professor Tony Warnes (Sheffield Institute for Studies on Ageing, University of Sheffield).

Finally we would like to thank our funding body, the Community Fund and in particular our current Grants Manager, Suzanne Candy, for her help and support.

A day in the life of a retirement community resident

Maud is a 73-year-old widow who moved to Berryhill Retirement Village a year after it opened. She moved with her husband from their nearby council house where they had lived for 48 years. They both had health concerns: he because of a stroke that had left him partially paralysed, and Maud because of recurrent chest infections and mild osteoarthritis. Her husband died soon after they moved in. Both Maud and her husband left school at 14. Maud had done part-time work as a typist/telephonist and her husband was a coal miner. She describes herself as moderately religious. Maud does not drive a car and relies on public transport during the day. If she goes out in the evening it is generally with her son or daughter.

Maud particularly valued the increased sense of safety and security she got from living in the village and felt that, were she to need it, more help would be available from staff. For now, however, she relied on her two children if she needed assistance with anything. Maud felt quite lonely at times in her first couple of years: in part this was because of the death of her husband, but it was also because she had never been the sort of person to make friends easily. She now feels that she has some good friends around her, but this had taken time. The following is an extract from Maud's diary:

> Wet and cold outside. Slept very well: so much better since I moved in here. It's a lovely feeling to know that there are others around you if you need them. After breakfast I phoned the doctor's for an appointment. My breathing hasn't been as good since the weather started closing in. They were able to fit me in tomorrow. After that, I took my washing downstairs and had a coffee while it was going through. There were a few of the regulars sat around and we had a good laugh. It's nice to look out and know you don't have to coat up and face into it. When the washing was sorted I went to the aerobics class. I often don't feel like making the effort, but generally feel so much better when I do. I had bad depression after my husband died and went to the hospital every day for a while. I feel so much better nowadays. The weather cheered up after lunch, so I decided to go into town to buy a new kettle. The bus service to Berryhill is much better now and it only took me half an hour door to door. While I was there, I thought I'd pick up some bits and pieces for the children for Christmas, always good to start early. When I was in the shopping centre I bumped into Mary and Fred, my old next-door neighbours. So we went for a cup of tea together. It was lovely to see them. They are thinking of moving themselves. Some lads threw a brick through their window last week and they say that you can see the drug dealers operating in broad daylight at the end of the road most days now. Things have changed so much since we were young families on the estate. I got back in time for the card class, which was very busy because we have a lot of orders for Christmas. One of the staff was taking names for the next trip, so I've put my name down. I promised her I'd think about the holiday they're arranging – but I'm not sure about the abseiling! ... she said I wouldn't have to do it if I didn't want to...
>
> After dinner, Tom the singer came, so I went down with some friends. He sang some nice tunes. It was a lovely couple of hours. I was in bed for about ten.

Retirement communities: the context

Introduction

Today, policy makers and providers are increasingly aware that housing and care services for older people need to be more flexible, innovative and inclusive. Developments designed to empower, provide choice and promote the autonomy of older people are being explored and encouraged (DoH, 2001; Peace and Holland, 2001; Riseborough, 2002). In Britain, one of the most recent developments is the creation of purpose-built retirement villages similar to those that have been around in North America and Europe for some time. The growing interest in such communities reflects both an awareness of the ageing of our population and a recognition that people are wanting more say in where and how they live, the design of their environments, and what kinds of care and support they might require in the future (Bernard and Phillips, 1998; Riseborough, 1998; Sumner, 2002). In addition, many middle-aged and older people are now actively exploring ways of developing new lifestyles and maintaining a positive identity in later life (Biggs, 1999a; Bernard et al, 2000). Retirement communities are particularly important in these regards not least because current social policy is promoting such developments as suitable for both 'fit' and 'frail' older people (ODPM, 2003). They also aim to create an environment that is intended to enhance a certain sort of ageing: one that is active, free of age prejudice and positive in its encouragement of certain forms of self-expression.

This report presents the findings of a three-year study (2000-03) which, though based on the experiences of people associated with one particular purpose-built retirement village: Berryhill in Stoke-on-Trent, was primarily designed to draw out the wider lessons for those who might be considering developing similar schemes. An earlier study had provided the managing organisation – The ExtraCare Charitable Trust – with a series of practice recommendations (Ray, 2001). Consequently, the focus of the present study was on what could be learnt more generally about how living in a new purpose-built retirement village affects the health, identity and well-being of residents. We were also interested in how people who work in, and have connections with, this kind of development perceive the growth of such communities for older people. A further underlying principle of the study, in keeping with the ethos of the funding body (the Community Fund) and of ExtraCare, was the notion of collaborative and participatory action research. We thus sought ways to include as many members of the Berryhill community as possible in developing and participating in all aspects of the study. One expected consequence of such an approach is that participants can directly influence the research and use it to help them determine their own, and the community's, future directions (Atkinson and Hammersley, 1994; Weisbord and Janoff, 1995).

Background

Who lives in purpose-built retirement communities?

Retirement communities are a relatively new long-term accommodation and care option in Britain. They first emerged in the North America of the 1950s but, since this time, there has been a great deal of debate about how to define such communities. Increasingly complex typologies have been produced but, basically, we can identify two broad types: communities that have been specifically constructed to meet the needs of older people – that is, purpose-built; and communities that have amassed concentrations of older people naturally through choice and through age-related migrations (Folts and Muir, 2002).

Research in Britain, Europe and North America has shown that existing purpose-built retirement communities are principally private rather than public or voluntary sector developments. They attract a mainly middle-class population from a wide geographical area; and higher incomes, owner occupation, good educational levels and good health are notable features (Bayley, 1996; Tulle-Winton, 2000; Croucher et al, 2003). They tend, moreover, to exclude minority ethnic groups (Kastenbaum, 1993) and are often people who have taken, and can afford to take, early retirement. In other words, residents form a selected group.

Health, identity and well-being among retirement community dwellers

In the US, where it is estimated that about five per cent of older Americans live in purpose-built retirement communities (Streib, 2002), there has been considerable concern about tailoring these environments to the leisure and lifestyle requirements of retired people. In continental Northern Europe by contrast, there has been a greater interest in the role of self-directed communities and continued collective participation. However, in both cases, these communities are characterised by age homogeneity and by claims that this enhances people's life satisfaction as well as their social, physical and mental well-being. Research also suggests that living in these environments helps to combat loneliness as well as improving morale and encouraging the development of healthier lifestyles (Hochschild, 1978; Longino and McLelland, 1978; Osgood, 1982; Lucksinger, 1994; Rodabough, 1994; Laws, 1995). For example, both men and women have been shown to increase their voluntary activity and membership of clubs after moving in, while men are more likely than women to engage in physical activity and exercise (Erickson et al, 2000; Resnick, 2001). Security and independence are also key attractions of such communities.

We also know that women outnumber men in retirement communities, but the proportions vary

from study to study. Some are comparable with the 2:1 proportion that one finds in community dwelling samples of older adults (Erickson et al, 2000) while others record figures as high as 8 or even 10:1, which are analogous to residential and nursing home studies (Resnick, 2001). Numerically, then, these are definitely female-dominated environments. Moreover, women who have never married or who are widowed also report that they are able to find more friends and that shared/mutual interests deepen these friendships (Madigan et al, 1996; Siegenthaler and Vaughan, 1998). This has led certain commentators to argue that having a majority of women (most of whom are widows) in such communities "sets the tone of the place" (Hochschild, 1978).

Criticisms of retirement communities

On the downside, critics such as the late Maggie Kuhn (1977) characterise retirement communities as "playpens for the old". Kastenbaum (1993) also highlighted how residents often see themselves as actively opting out from wider society and developing aggressively age-conscious identities. Furthermore, he and Glenda Laws (1995) noted a tendency for residents to criticise other older people who maintain intergenerational links such as grandparenting, and to exclude residents should their levels of mental or physical incapacity upset the image of a 'positively' ageing community. The rhetoric of positive and active ageing may also place considerable pressure on residents to conform to this image, although their experience may vary considerably from this expectation (Biggs et al, 2000). A related contention is that age-segregated retirement communities may in fact produce 'ghettos' of increasing dependency and service demand (Kuhn, 1977).

From a policy perspective, British interest in these developments has centred on their value as a positive alternative to traditional forms of residential and nursing home care. While it appears that the number of British retirement communities is growing, there are, as yet, no nationally collated statistics specifically related to this trend. Nor do we know if the findings from North American and European research apply in a British context. It was with these policy issues and questions in mind that our study sought to explore what it was like to live and work in one new purpose-built retirement village – Berryhill.

The study and the report

The study was guided by four overarching research questions (see Appendix A):

- What effect does the environment of Berryhill have on residents' well-being?
- What is the perceived health status of residents in Berryhill?
- How is a retirement community like Berryhill related to ageing identities and what strategies do residents adopt towards significant others?
- How do stakeholders view life at Berryhill?

Beyond this, the intention was to examine the contribution that this new model of accommodation and care could make to improving the lives of older people, drawing out the wider implications for those who may wish to develop such retirement communities in the future.

In the report that follows, the research questions are addressed over the course of five different chapters. In the remainder of Chapter 1 we give brief details about how the study was carried out together with a portrait of Berryhill Retirement Village and the people who lived and worked there at the start of the study. This sets the context for the more detailed exploration of health, identity and well-being in succeeding chapters. In Chapter 2, the focus is on the first research question and we explore how participation and involvement in village life can contribute to people's sense of well-being and the development of a new lifestyle. Chapter 3 develops the discussion of well-being by expanding this to consider what residents and others say about health, about help and support, and how these may, or may not, have changed over time (research question two). Chapter 4 concentrates on the third research question, exploring age and identity and how people feel about themselves now they are living in this new environment. Maintaining a positive identity in later life is a complex issue and combines aspects of health, psychological well-being and the social environment considered earlier in the report. Finally, in Chapter 5, we draw together a number of key issues that have arisen during the course of the study and reflect on their implications.

Each of the three central chapters (2, 3 and 4) take one of the first three research questions as its major focus. Additionally, every chapter considers the views of stakeholders (research question four) in order to present a more rounded picture of some of the ways in which Berryhill relates to the surrounding community and how different groups view life in the village. Because the study was conducted over a three-year period, change over time is a crucial dimension of health, identity and well-being. Consequently, this too is considered in each of the three central chapters.

Readers may wonder about some of the terminology used in the report. During the course of the study, we found that people who lived in Berryhill often used different terms from those used by staff or professional stakeholders. For example, they repeatedly referred to themselves as 'residents', rather than tenants (although technically this is what they are). We therefore use the term 'residents' throughout. Similarly, residents would consistently talk about being 'on' or 'off care' although, officially, they receive 'packages of support' (see later in this chapter). In this instance, the report makes use of the terms 'upport package' or 'support services'. Although the majority of staff are employed as Resident Support Workers (RSWs) they, and the residents, always use the word 'carers', so this is how they are referred to within the report.

Furthermore, as will become evident, Berryhill caters for a range of people in terms of age, abilities, health status and so on. For the purposes of analysis and reporting, we present, where relevant, comparative data along a number of major dimensions such as gender, marital status, or whether or not people are in receipt of support services. The study was not designed to make direct comparisons with other forms of accommodation and care in later life. A new study is underway elsewhere with this as its focus[1]. Where appropriate, however, we draw on existing literature to support or counter the findings presented here. Finally, although the local social services department commissions intensive support for a number of their clients who live in Berryhill, the study, and this report, did not set out to compare this group of people with everyone else living there.

[1] Funded by the Joseph Rowntree Foundation, the study aims to assess the strengths and weaknesses of different models of providing housing and care for older people by comparing Hartrigg Oaks Continuing Care Retirement Community with five other case studies. Professor Bernard is a member of the Project Advisory Group.

A reframing of the research questions, and a reanalysis of the data, would be required for this purpose.

How the study was carried out

The study began on a part-time basis in June 2000, two years after Berryhill Retirement Village first opened in May 1998. A multi-method, participatory action research approach was adopted, using a number of different, but interrelated strategies to gather data and information over the course of the three years. As Figure 1.1 shows, the study encompassed informal methods such as participant observation as well as highly structured techniques

such as the administration of three waves of questionnaires to residents (see also Appendices B and C)[2].

It is also important to note here that in order to explore health, identity and well-being, a number of existing and well-validated tools were used that are referred to throughout this report. These are summarised in Figure 1.2.

---

[2] A separate technical report provides details and examples of all the tools and schedules which were used, together with information about response rates, attrition rates and ethical issues.

Figure 1.1: Summary of timeline and research methods used

	From June 2000	2001	2002	To Oct 2003
Participant observation	Ongoing	ongoing	ongoing	until Sept
Existing documentation	Ongoing	ongoing	ongoing	ongoing
Resident questionnaires		Feb-June	Feb-May	Feb-April
Participation groups and community conferences	April-Nov	Nov	until Sept	
Individual and group stakeholder interviews	from Nov	ongoing	until April	
Diaries		from Feb	ongoing	until April
Family/friends questionnaires				March
Staff questionnaires				Feb

Berryhill: Main entrance to the village

Figure 1.2: Tools used in the study

The Short Form 12 (Ware and Sherbourne, 1992)
- a scale to assess physical and mental health;
- assesses eight dimensions of health: physical functioning, mental health, social functioning, role limitations because of physical problems, role limitations because of mental problems, energy/vitality, pain and general health perceptions;
- scores are calculated on a scale from 0 (worst possible health) to 100 (best possible health);
- two summary scores, the physical component summary (PCS) and the mental component summary (MCS), can be calculated.

The Diener Satisfaction with Life Scale (Diener et al, 1985)
- a scale to assess well-being;
- has five items/statements;
- respondents say how much they agree with each statement;
- each statement is scored from one to seven, so that the range of scores is 5 (low satisfaction) through to 35 (highly satisfied).

CASP-19 (Hyde et al, 2003)
- a scale to assess well-being and quality of life;
- has 19 items/statements with four domains: **C**ontrol, **A**utonomy, **S**elf-realisation, and **P**leasure;
- respondents say how often they feel the way described in the statement;
- scores range from 0 (total absence of quality of life) through to 57 (total satisfaction on all four domains).

We also developed a social masking scale (see Biggs et al, 2002) and used Oberg and Tornstam's (1999) age satisfaction questions to look at identity issues.

In addition to the methods and tools noted earlier, formal channels of communication were established for the ongoing exchange of information between the research team and our collaborating organisation. Regular Liaison Group meetings took place every two months between the village management, a representative of ExtraCare and the research team. We also kept in routine contact with staff in person, on the phone and via e-mail. A project Advisory Group met bi-annually and included two residents, the manager of the village and her assistant manager, representatives from ExtraCare and Touchstone Housing Association (the developers), personnel from the local social services department and NHS Trust, and two external academic colleagues. A monthly column entitled 'Keele Gossip' also became a regular feature in the village newsletter.

Throughout this report, we draw on both quantitative and qualitative data from the three years of the study. We try to make explicit which wave or waves of quantitative data we are referring to as appropriate. On occasion, we also talk about the 'core group'. These are the respondents who completed all three waves of the resident questionnaires (54 in total). In addition, where quotations are used, pseudonyms have been employed in order to protect the identity of participants in the study.

Berryhill Retirement Village: a profile

Berryhill accommodates people over the age of 55 and is located in a deprived urban area (DoH, 2000) adjacent to the large 1950s Bentilee council housing estate. However, it also has a rural feel to it because it is sited on the edge of a previous opencast coalmine that is now parkland (Berryhill Fields). The village is at the top of a long incline, below which are Berryhill junior school and high school, as well as a small number of shops including a chemist and a supermarket. The village itself is a single, three-storey, T-shaped building containing 148 flats along a series of internal 'streets'. The flats consist of a bedroom, sitting room, hallway, kitchen and bathroom. All bedrooms and sitting rooms face outwards; the kitchen windows and front doors open onto the internal streets. All flats are suitable for wheelchair users, all have allocated parking spaces and those on the ground floor have small garden areas accessed via French windows.

All the flats are rented and residents either live independently or are on one of four different levels of support package (Figure 1.3). All residents receiving a support service are visited daily and, if they wish, residents can also purchase help with housekeeping, shopping, pension collection and laundry.

Figure 1.3: Levels of support provided to residents

Level 1	Someone able to live in their own home in the community, needing minimal support, perhaps two to three calls a week, pension collection, perhaps help with a bath
Level 2	As above, still able to live in their own home but with two or three calls a day, perhaps in the morning and the evening
Level 3	The individual would normally move into mainstream residential care, requiring up to four calls a day, assistance at the main times, such as meal times, getting up, going to bed, and so on
Level 4	Very dependent individual, needing help as above but during the night as well, that is, visits every three to four hours during a 24-hour period. Stops short of nursing care

Berryhill has a variety of facilities for the use of residents including a gym and jacuzzi, craft, woodwork and computer rooms, a village hall, restaurant and bar area, a small shop, hairdresser and library, and a greenhouse and communal gardens. Importantly, these facilities and their associated activities are not routinely found in other more traditional forms of accommodation and care for older people. There is a public telephone in the building but residents can also install telephones in their own flats.

The flats themselves are fitted with emergency bell cords in each room and all residents are issued with 'OK signs'. These signs say 'I'm OK' on one side, and 'I'm not well, please knock' on the other. Residents are expected to hang the cards on the outside of their front doors each morning. If no card is visible when staff go round to check, they will knock and, if necessary, enter the flat to ensure that the resident is all right. In addition to the 'I'm OK' cards, residents can request a daily call. The building itself is accessed via an electronic entrance system that, together with CCTV viewable by residents on their television sets, allows them to admit their own visitors. Internally there are locked doors to each wing, accessible only to residents and staff. However, certain regular visitors, such as some GPs, have a swipe card that lets them in through the front door but does not give them access to the rest of the village.

New residents are provided with a Welcome Pack that includes details of the facilities and activities available at Berryhill. Most of these have a charge attached. A social club, which has resident and non-resident members, also operates. The original programme of activities was developed by the residents themselves through a series of Vision Workshops. These were first run in advance of opening Berryhill and are now run approximately

every other year. In the interim, the activity programme evolves through the creation of interest groups who meet together to identify the ways and means needed to establish any new activity. One member of staff acts as an Activities Coordinator and supports these various groups. To further promote resident participation, monthly street meetings are held throughout the village. These meetings are used by management to feed back any action taken over the past month, to inform people of upcoming events and to encourage residents to voice any concerns or complaints they might have. Other information is conveyed by means of notice boards, the monthly village news-sheet and an in-house television service. There are also many opportunities for residents to volunteer their services in a variety of roles both within, and beyond, Berryhill.

Living and working in Berryhill Retirement Village

We turn now to consider some basic details about the people who live and work in the village. This information is drawn from what we know about the total resident population at the start of the study, from documents and from the first annual questionnaire completed by residents in the spring of 2001.

Who lives in Berryhill Retirement Village?

In the spring of 2001, there were 159 residents of whom two thirds were women (109; 69%) and a third were men (50; 31%). All the residents were white British. Berryhill and ExtraCare identify four age categories in their attempt to maintain an even distribution of ages: 55-65, 65-75, 75-85 and 85+. For the purposes of comparative analysis, we have slightly altered these groups so that there is no overlap. The data in Table 1.1 show that the age

Table 1.1: Ages of Berryhill residents and questionnaire respondents

	age 55-64		age 65-74		age 75-84		age 85+		Total	
	n	(%)	n	(%)	n	(%)	n	(%)	n	(%)
Whole village	15	(9)	55	(35)	71	(45)	18	(11)	159	(100)
Questionnaire	6	(7)	33	(38)	39	(44)	10	(11)	88	(100)

profile of the 88 people who responded to the Wave 1 questionnaire, is very close to the village as a whole.

Moreover, although the village can and does accommodate very elderly people (the oldest resident was aged 91), only one in ten residents are in fact over the age of 85. This contrasts markedly with sheltered housing and with residential and nursing home environments, where 20% of residents are aged 85 and over (Age Concern, 2003). This disparity is also reflected in the fact that the average age of village residents remained at 75/76 over the three years (for both women and men) while, in Britain, it is currently 85 for those residing in residential homes (Netten et al, 2001).

From the existing data available in Berryhill at the beginning of the study, it was not possible to

accurately establish, for example, the marital situation or health status of residents. This information only became available towards the end of the study with the research team assisting in the development of a computerised database. Residents' health status and support levels are reported on in detail in Chapter 3.

However, at the start of the study, it was possible to determine who lived alone or who lived with another person. Not unexpectedly, the majority of residents (111; 70%) lived alone and, as Figure 1.4 shows, there were also clear gender differences: half of the men (25; 50%) were living with another person compared with only one in five of the women (23; 21%). This is very different from figures available for the living arrangements of older people in the wider community. In England, 81% of men and 63% of women in the 65-74 age group live with

Berryhill: Main street and main entrance

Photograph by Stephen W. Ellis

Figure 1.4: Living arrangements by gender: whole village

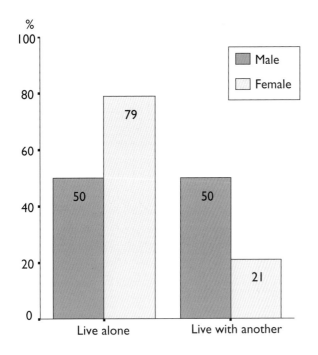

Figure 1.5: Living arrangements by gender (Wave 1)

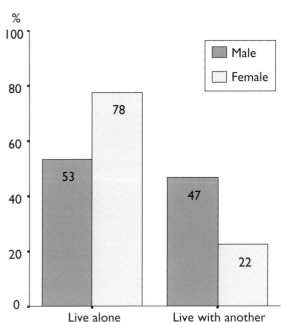

another person; over the age of 75, this reduces to 66% of men and 40% of women (Age Concern, 2003).

Figure 1.5 again shows that those who responded to the Wave 1 questionnaire accurately reflected the population of the village as a whole in terms of their living arrangements.

Data from the Wave 1 questionnaire did enable us to determine the marital status of respondents. Given the observations earlier in this chapter about living arrangements, it is not surprising to find that the majority of respondents were widowed (see Figure 1.6) and that, once again, there were some marked gender differences (see Figure 1.7).

Nearly half the male respondents were married or cohabiting (14; 46%) in comparison with only a quarter of the women (15; 26%). Moreover, only one man (3%) was divorced, compared with six women (10%), while two women had never married. As one would expect, more women (35; 60%) than men (15; 50%) were widowed. However, while this remained consistent over the three years of the study, it is important to note that the marital status figures in the general community dwelling population of older people are markedly different (Age Concern,

2003). Here, only 9% of men aged between 65 and 74, and 29% over 75 are widowed, compared with 27% and 70% respectively for men in these age groups in Berryhill. For women, the comparable figures are 31% of those aged between 65 and 74 and 61% of those over 75, compared with 50% and 76.5% respectively for women in Berryhill.

Furthermore, those who responded to the Wave 1 questionnaire all moved from within a 10-mile radius and about one third of them (31; 35%) in fact came from the immediate vicinity. Connected with this, the majority of people moved to Berryhill from rented accommodation (52; 59%) while about one third came from their own property (27; 30%). Another five (6%) people moved from local sheltered housing. Four people did not specify.

The principal reasons people gave for moving to the village are shown in Table 1.2. While moving decisions are often complex and getting on for one third of people gave more than one reason (27; 29%) it was their own, or their partner's health, that was by far the most important factor.

The area in which Berryhill is located is ranked sixth highest out of 376 local and unitary authorities in England and Wales for no qualifications (ONS, 2001).

Figure 1.6: Marital status (Wave 1)

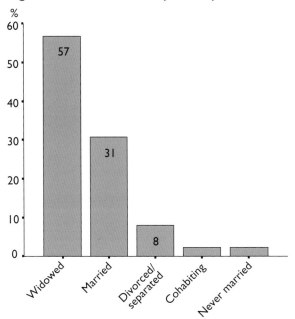

Figure 1.7: Marital status by gender (Wave1)

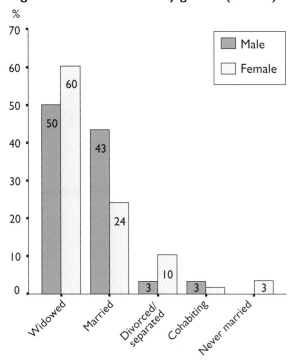

It was therefore not surprising to find that nine out of ten respondents left school at or before the age of 15 (74; 93%). There were no significant gender differences although a third of the men (nine; 32%) compared with a fifth of the women (11; 19%) said they left education after primary school. Only one man and one woman had gone on to college or university. Three out of four respondents had been employed in manual occupations (72; 75%), for example, in the mining, steel and pottery industries, while only 10 people (10%) were in non-manual employment such as secretarial or postal work. Fourteen women (14%) listed their previous occupation as housewife.

Who works in Berryhill Retirement Village?

Currently, there are 38 members of staff (average age 38) who, between them, cover the village 24 hours a day, 365 days a year. This has increased substantially from the original complement of 23. Aside from the Manager and Assistant Manager, staff work in teams comprising a team leader and four or five Resident Support Workers (often called 'carers' by the residents). Staff work variable hours and, as well as a system of allocation of residents with support needs, there is a key worker system in place for all residents (not just those receiving support). Each key worker is responsible for approximately 10 residents at any one time. Three members of staff cover the village at

night: one sleeping in, and two who are awake and carry out housekeeping responsibilities. In addition, there are three kitchen staff, a well-being nurse, a gym instructor, an activities coordinator, a part-time administrator and a part-time bookkeeper. A member of the Directorate of ExtraCare acts as a link person with Berryhill.

During the three years of the study, there were only two male Resident Support Workers. From the questionnaires completed by staff, it was evident that almost all of them had previous experience of working with older people. All staff (except the newest recruits) are trained to NVQ Level 2 as a minimum and two were qualified as nurses. Following induction, staff can access an extensive programme of training including statutory training (such as first aid, moving and handling, food and hygiene and so on), the Kaizen training system to aid problem solving, and leadership training for team leaders. Staff can also access other external training opportunities and they keep personal achievement logs. The management team have monthly support visits from a member of the Directorate, and away days three times a year. Staff said that they were generally satisfied with their job, giving it an average score of seven out of ten. However, although the staff provide valued and valuable support (see Chapter 3), many of them viewed the work as a job to be done rather than as a vocation and, aside from

Table 1.2: Principal reason for moving to Berryhill Retirement Village by gender and age (Wave 2)

| | Gender | | | | Age | | | | | | |
| | Male | | Female | | Up to 75 | | 76+ | | Total | |
	n	(%)	n	(%)	n	(%)	n	(%)	n	(%)
Own health	6	(26)	30	(43)	12	(28)	24	(48)	36	(39)
Partner's health	3	(13)	4	(6)	4	(9)	3	(6)	7	(8)
House/garden too big	4	(17)	12	(17)	10	(23)	6	(12)	16	(17)
Security	7	(31)	5	(7)	7	(16)	5	(10)	12	(13)
Social opportunities	0	(0)	2	(3)	0	(0)	2	(4)	2	(2)
Death of spouse	0	(0)	6	(9)	4	(9)	2	(4)	6	(6)
Other reasons	2	(9)	10	(14)	6	(14)	6	(12)	12	(13)
Don't know	1	(4)	1	(1)	0	(0)	2	(4)	2	(2)
Total	23	(100)	70	(100)	43	(100)	50	(100)	93	(100)

the management team, declined to be interviewed for the study.

Aside from the staff, Berryhill also has a number of outside volunteers who help to run the classes, manage the bar and the shop, and who accompany less well residents on trips. These 50 or so outside volunteers include family members and friends, as well as local residents and people seeking work experience.

Conclusion

This opening chapter has established the context for our exploration of health, identity and well-being in subsequent chapters. However, even from the brief profile given earlier, it is evident that Berryhill demonstrates both similarities and differences with regard to existing research. A major difference from studies in North America is that Berryhill accommodates a predominantly working-class clientele, many of whom have moved in from the local area, are widowed and now living alone. Given that it also caters for people from the age of 55 to over 90, it is difficult to argue, as North American research has done, that this is an age homogeneous community. However, like other retirement community studies, Berryhill also contains an exclusively white population, women outnumber men, and health and security are important reasons why people move to such an environment in later life.

There is, therefore, a potential tension between homogeneity and diversity, and maintaining a balance between the different generations in the village and between those who are independent and those who require support of various kinds will continue to be key challenges for the future. Moreover, as we shall

see in greater detail in the next chapter, residents are encouraged to participate in village life through the provision of various activities and facilities and there is an emphasis on becoming actively involved in the community. Linked with this are issues about how residents perceive staff and how staff respond to them and to the needs raised by a population who, while they are being encouraged to age well, are at the same time ageing and dying 'in place'. The qualifications and skills of staff, what is expected of them, and the implications for ongoing training and support are crucial here.

Summary

- Purpose-built retirement villages like Berryhill are a relatively new development in Britain. They are being portrayed as a positive alternative to traditional forms of residential and nursing home care yet we do not know if the findings from North American and European research apply equally here.
- This study explored the effect that the development of Berryhill had on residents, their families, staff, helping agencies and other stakeholders in the surrounding community, looking particularly at aspects of health, identity and well-being. It adopted a multi-method, participatory action research approach, using a number of different, but interrelated strategies to gather data and information over three years (2000-03). The information has been used to examine the contribution this new model of accommodation and care can make to improving the lives of older people, and to draw out the wider implications for those who may wish to develop such communities in the future.
- Berryhill Retirement Village is located on the edge of a deprived urban area and is a single,

three-storey, T-shaped building containing 148 rented flats along a series of internal 'streets'. Residents either live independently or are on one of four different levels of support package. There is a pervading ethos of participation and involvement that is facilitated by the provision of a social club, a programme of activities, a range of on-site facilities, monthly street meetings, a monthly village news-sheet and an in-house television service. There are also many opportunities for residents to volunteer their services in a variety of roles both within, and beyond, the village.

- At the start of the study, Berryhill accommodated 159 people over the age of 55. It consists of an exclusively white population and women outnumber men in a ratio of 2:1. The majority of residents (111; 70%) live alone (79% of women and 50% of men). The average age of village residents is 75/76.

- 88 of the 159 residents completed a Wave 1 questionnaire (a response rate of 55%). Half the men were married/cohabiting and half were widowed. Three out of five women (60%) were widowed, a quarter were married (26%), six (10%) were divorced and two (4%) had never married.

- Health-related issues (affecting oneself or one's partner) were the prime reason that people had moved into Berryhill.

- Nine out of ten respondents left school at or before the age of 15 and three quarters had been employed in manual occupations in, for example, the mining, steel and pottery industries. Ten respondents had undertaken non-manual employment such as secretarial or postal work and 14 women gave 'housewife' as their previous occupation.

- Berryhill is run by a team of 38 staff. They work variable hours but cover the village 24 hours a day, 365 days a year. A system of allocation of residents with support needs operates and there is a key-worker system for all residents. Three members of staff cover the village at night, and there are three kitchen staff, a well-being nurse, a gym instructor, a part-time administrator and a part-time bookkeeper.

2

Developing a retirement community lifestyle: participation and involvement

Introduction

This chapter turns the spotlight on the means by which older people are enabled to play a part in actively creating a new retirement village lifestyle for themselves. Retirement communities like Berryhill are centrally concerned with the well-being and quality of life of residents. One way in which this is addressed is through encouraging and facilitating the participation and involvement of people in village life in particular, and community life more generally. Drawing on both qualitative and quantitative data, this chapter explores:

- use of and satisfaction with the village and its amenities;
- activities and interest groups;
- getting out and about;
- volunteering;
- contact with family and friends;
- democratic decision making.

It considers who participates in activities, what benefits residents gain from their involvement, and what some of the barriers to further participation might be. We look too at how some of these aspects have changed and modified over time, and at what

Berryhill: The Greenhouse

stakeholders think about these features of retirement community living.

Village amenities: use and satisfaction

Chapter 1 showed that residents have access to a wide variety of on-site amenities, most of which are not routinely found in traditional forms of accommodation and care for older people. In the questionnaires, we asked people to tell us whether they knew about and used 14 of the amenities and, if so, how satisfied they were with them.

Table 2.1 shows that respondents who used the amenities rated them all very highly, giving them an average satisfaction score of at least 8 out of 10 (10 = completely satisfied). There were no differences in satisfaction scores between men and women. The hairdresser, restaurant, shop and bar are the most well-known amenities and were used consistently by between half and two thirds of respondents over the three years of the study. These amenities are all located off the main street in the village. Consequently, they are visible and easily accessible settings for people to meet and mix informally.

Most of the other facilities were only used by small numbers of people even if they knew of them. For example, about one in five respondents used the gym, while use of the craft room dropped from two in five, to one in five over the three years. Less than one in ten people used the woodwork, dreamscape (relaxation) and computer rooms. The two exceptions to this were the library and the gardens.

By the end of the study, the library was being used by a third of respondents while the use of the gardens had gone up considerably to three out of five people. A refurbishment programme together with relocation of the vegetable garden may well have been contributory factors here.

Furthermore, a proportion of respondents claimed not to know about certain amenities despite everyone receiving details in their Welcome Pack when they arrive. The dreamscape room, the Well-being Project (which was fairly new at the time of the Wave 2 questionnaire) and the visitor's flat were the least known about.

This suggests that there may be some issues both around communicating with and informing people about what is available, as well as who actually uses certain amenities, points we return to in the concluding chapter of this report. Over and above these individual amenities, the majority of respondents were extremely satisfied both with their flat and with the village as a whole. On average the flats received a score of 10 out of 10 at Wave 2 (Wave 1=10; Wave 3=9.5), as did the village itself (Wave 1=9; Wave 3=9).

Activities and interest groups

Over its lifetime, many interest groups have been formed at Berryhill and many activities initiated and organised by residents. Analysis of the Wave 2 questionnaire, shows which on-site activities respondents regarded as most important in their lives (Table 2.2). For the women, arts and crafts and keep fit top their activities list. For the men, keep fit and

Table 2.1: Satisfaction with amenities in Berryhill Retirement Village (Wave 2)

	Average score (max=10)	Range	*n* Know/use and rated	*n* Don't use	*n* Don't know about
Hairdresser	10	5-10	56	36	2
Craft	10	2-10	20	72	1
Gym	10	7-10	18	75	1
Visitor's flat	10	6-10	15	63	13
Dreamscape room	10	8-10	5	63	25
Library	9	5-10	33	62	0
Gardens	9	5-10	27	66	2
Well-being Project	9	7-10	15	59	19
Greenhouse	9	5-10	11	81	1
Computer	9	7-10	8	84	3
Shop	8	2-10	45	45	3
Restaurant	8	1-10	42	50	2
Bar	8	2-10	42	47	3
Woodwork	8	5-9	7	85	4

Table 2.2: Most important activities at Berryhill (Wave 2)

	Male	Female	Total
Arts and crafts	1	14	15
Keep fit	2	12	14
Dancing	1	4	5
Bingo	1	4	5
Entertainment	0	4	4
Volunteer/ambassador	1	3	4
Other	9	7	16
Total	15	48	63

computing (under the 'other' category) were most important. Residents took part in an average of four activities in and around the village.

The provision and availability of on-site activities and facilities were crucially linked with transportation and security issues. At all three waves of the questionnaire, the vast majority of respondents said that they felt safe while out and about in the village (Wave 1=97%; Wave 2=100%; Wave 3=99%). This was a welcome contrast with the lives many of them had led previously, as participants in an early conference planning group explain:

Facilitator: "Do you think you would be doing those sorts of things if you didn't live here?"

All: "No."

Kathleen: "Definitely not."

Margaret: "I would never go out at night when I hadn't come in here."

Patricia: "Inside at 4 o'clock and the doors and windows locked up tight, that was how it was, wasn't it?"

Margaret: "You might join a pensioners club like they have at the school and that.... "

Patricia: "But you would go one afternoon but not at night.... But here you are sort of going out but you haven't got to go outside the building, have you? You come down for entertainment. It's like you are going out but you haven't got to go out in the cold or a taxi and you're alright."

This emphasis on activity, active participation and their connections with well-being were reflected

from many different viewpoints, not least in ExtraCare's publicity material which states:

Activities – they are at the heart of everything we do. Activity transforms residents' lifestyles and staff lifestyles alike. But activity, both physical and mental, not only keeps older people fitter, it also helps even the frailest of residents regain abilities they thought were gone forever.

One of the developers also made a clear link between activities, facilities and the provision of support:

"It was the lifestyle issue that particularly appealed to me ...: what you built into it, and the ... range of spaces that can be used for a variety of practical activities, hence the shop, the concert hall, the pub, the restaurant, the craftwork room, the woodwork room and so on; and then the fitness centre and so on.... The second strand was then the care package.... The third strategy was the activity, was the social side."

These kinds of statements were endorsed by residents, who frequently referred to on-site activities as a major element of their new lifestyle:

Enid: "I was going to say: we all go aerobics twice a week."

Tina: "We enjoy that."

Alice: "Yes. I go in the gym on Mondays. Then on Monday night I sit there tapping my toes and watching the dance."

Enid: "You don't have to be bored and lonely really, do you?"

Bea: "If I'd got to get a bus to town to go to aerobics, I wouldn't dream of it. I come down here and quite enjoy it. Some days you think, 'Oh I don't think I can cope today, I'm not feeling too good', you come down and you feel so much better for it."

Family and friends also mentioned the activities and village facilities as an important attraction, while other stakeholder groups such as the following hospital social workers talked positively about the opportunities for social interaction:

Joan: " ... seeing someone going in to that sort [of] environment ... there's a number of aspects they are actually looking for: the level of care, ... the security aspect and the social aspect. So it's very often that six weeks down the line – which is when we do our review – that there is often a noticeable change in that person's view. Socially they've been able to make friends which has given them a whole new sort of outlook on life. And physically."

Craig: "I would tend to agree with that, yes."

David: " ... from my conversation with the people who live there, they seem quite happy there and they've been able to make new friends and they know exactly where everything is ... I felt that they thought that they fitted in somewhere.... "

And here, managers from the local social services department compare Berryhill with residential care, highlighting the ways in which activities contribute to challenging and raising the expectations of residents:

Mel: "[in comparison with residential care] ... they have far more opportunities."

Jane: "Far more opportunities."

Mel: "Absolutely, oh yes. We couldn't offer that level of support in a residential home."

Jane: "The idea of people striving to do something different, the sort of fostering of ambition I thought was a very positive thing to do."

Getting out and about

Taking part in activities available at Berryhill is one way in which people are enabled to fashion a new lifestyle for themselves; getting out and about, maintaining links with the surrounding area and with the people who live there, is another important facet. This again raises the twin issues of transport and security and it comes as no surprise to find that seven out of ten respondents do not in fact own a car (69; 71%). Gender differences were also evident with just over half of male respondents owning a car (13; 54%) in comparison with only one in five of the women (15; 21%). While nationally available figures on this issue relate to holding a current driving license (*Social Trends*, 2003), nonetheless it would seem that these

figures are lower than one would expect for community dwelling older people where 69% of men and 25% of women over the age of 70 hold a driving licence.

This means that most village residents were reliant on other forms of transport to get out and about. Two fifths of respondents got lifts from other people. These were predominantly family members and, most usually, a son or daughter. Bus and walking were the next most popular ways of getting around, with smaller numbers of people using taxis, dial-a-ride or voluntary transport schemes. Although there had been teething problems with the bus service early on, these seem to have been resolved by the time this study ended and those who used the service gave it an average satisfaction score of eight out of ten. Taxis on the other hand had often proved unreliable, and many people had given up using them.

Despite some difficulties with transport, many people went out on their own during the day. In fact, nearly three quarters of those who were completely independent went out (46; 73%) in contrast with only a third of those who received support (12; 38%). Most people also said that they felt safe in the neighbourhood outside the village although, over the three years of the study, the proportion saying this

Berryhill: Front of building and car park

Photograph by Stephen W. Ellis

went down (Wave 1=72%; Wave 2=67%; Wave 3=62%). There were no differences between men and women on the issue of feeling safe, although rather more women than men did not go out alone during the day (30 women [41%] compared with seven men [29%]). Moreover, those who did not go out alone during the day were significantly older (average 77.1 years) than those who did (average 73.6 years). Going out at night, however, was a different matter. Nine out of ten people said that they did not go out alone (84; 88%). Of those who did, nine were men, and just four were women.

Although substantial numbers of people do go out of the village, they regarded very few off-site activities as important in their lives: three women nominated clubs and bingo while for three of the men fishing was important. Only four people on support packages nominated any outside activities as important. There is, however, a popular and active trips interest group that, over the three years of the study, arranged outings on the Orient Express, to the races, to historic houses, garden centres and shopping malls. There have also been opportunities for residents of all abilities to go on adventure holidays and some have been on the tall-ships race. These trips were rated very highly indeed, receiving an average satisfaction score of ten out of ten. They are also key to the active and challenging ethos of the village as encapsulated by this member of staff:

> Angie: "It's a completely different feel to a nursing home. [When I worked there] I always compared them to lost souls.... Here it feels more alive. There are expectations and I think hope as well. When people say, 'I flew in a helicopter', or, 'I climbed that wall', or, 'I'm going on the Orient Express', there is expectation, and I think the learning curve, from the little that I've seen is, 'If she can do it, I can do it'. So it goes further and further."

Volunteering

As well as getting out and about, a related aspect of developing a new lifestyle concerns opportunities for volunteering. At any one time, there were about 60 resident volunteers, of whom 15 acted as volunteer ambassadors. Being an ambassador for Berryhill involved going out to meet others interested in setting up similar communities in other parts of the country, as well as showing visitors around their own village:

> Alice: "Well in here when you say ambassador, you mean someone who explains when visitors come round: give your time to showing them round and talking to them, answering their questions and doing what you can to help...."

> Maura: "It is taking people round, explaining, showing the village to them.... Telling them everything that goes on...."

> Alice: "You're not under pressure to, 'You mustn't tell them this', and 'You mustn't tell them that' – you're free to tell them, you're free to answer their questions from your own point of view."

> Kathleen: "And Maura and I go all round the place, well all over the country really."

The dedicated and enthusiastic work of volunteers and ambassadors was key to the functioning of the village. As well as ambassadors, there were also volunteer residents who managed the shop; worked in the greenhouse and gardens; organised raffles and other fund-raising activities; ran dance and art classes; and welcomed visitors at the front desk. Staff, family and friends also involved themselves in various ways: staff put on popular annual shows, while outside volunteers ran the café bar as well as certain other activities such as the art group.

Over the course of the study, a number of issues were raised in connection with volunteering and being an ambassador. For example, volunteers did not want to be taken for granted and were clear that there were certain limits to what they were able or willing to do. They were comfortable voicing their concerns but wanted these acknowledged and recognised:

> Margaret: "Yes. If you are asked to do things you can say no. I mean, if you are going out you just can't do it, or.... If I'm in and I want to do things I do it. But, I have refused a few times when I haven't been able to do it. You know, things they've asked, not with other residents, things we do for the village like showing people round or going somewhere you know."

> Kathleen: "That's alright if they let you know in advance about showing people round but when

they just ring you and say, 'Can you come down and show some visitors around', that's a bit off that is."

Further, the need to sustain and recruit more volunteers – both from inside the village and from outside – was a recurrent issue.

Contact with family and friends

Friends and family are important at all ages, and making and having the company of friends in the village was a crucial aspect of maintaining one's well-being and identity, as will be seen in Chapters 3 and 4. But, what becomes of one's involvement with friends and family when one moves into a new environment like this?

From the questionnaires, two thirds or more of respondents said they retained friends outside Berryhill (Wave 1=75%; Wave 2=65%; Wave 3=69%). Of those who maintained outside friendships, almost three out of five people said they were close or very close to their friends and that there was no conflict or tension between them. These figures were stable over the three waves of questionnaires and showed no differences between men and women. The majority of people also said they were very satisfied indeed with their outside friendships, scoring an average of nine out of ten at Wave 2, and ten out of ten at Wave 3.

In discussion, it was also clear that external friendships were maintained both through face-to-face contact and, importantly, via the telephone, as has been noted in other research (Phillipson et al, 2001). Here are participants at the second community conference talking about this:

> Bea: " ... in the wintertime you don't always go out but, if you have friends you're happy and content. You can keep in touch by telephone and by writing, but you don't sort of visit the same...."

> Janet: " ... I just keep in touch by 'phone with most of my friends now. I don't mix with those other friends as much, but we just keep in touch. I don't think you can...."

> Alice: "I see my old neighbours about once every two weeks. My two friends, my two oldest friends – unfortunately, one's 89 [laugh] and one is 85. We

keep in touch. My daughter will talk for hours on the 'phone."

> Facilitator: "So would you say that the 'phone is important?... "

> Bea: "It's got more important for me because I used to go to church regularly and I can't get, so some of those friends keep in contact by 'phone and exchanging cards."

Many people also maintained regular connections with their families. Data from the annual questionnaires revealed that, for seven out of ten respondents, family remained their main source of help (65; 71%, Wave 2). Moreover, from the family/friends questionnaires, it was evident that the majority visit the village once a week or more (27; 84%). When asked to score retirement villages as places to live, family and friends gave an average score of eight out of ten.

While some residents had a great deal of contact with their families, there were differing expectations about whether, or to what extent, families should stay involved with Berryhill once someone had moved in. For their part, residents emphasised how families had their own lives to lead, and how their being resident in the village was often important in lifting the emotional burden from families:

> Esther: "The beauty of it here is that your children come in it and can see it, can't they?"

> Moira: "Yes."

> Agnes: "And as soon as if you are ill or anything they let them know and things like that, don't they?"

> Cynthia: "Your family has more peace of mind...."

> Esther: "My daughter would call often because she didn't know what it was like, but now she will ring, she doesn't call, perhaps once a week now."

There was also a related concern about the extent of family involvement with the village more widely. Despite some residents being individually well supported, staff felt that family participation was generally lacking, particularly once people were in receipt of support packages. Like recruitment of volunteers, this was something staff felt needed to be continually addressed:

> Kerry: "But then you get the other side of the coin. You get somebody whose daughter will take the morning off to take them to hospital and wouldn't dream of asking a member of staff to take them."

> Angie: "I think it always has been in a sort of balance. There are some who care and some who don't ... but once they're on care the expectations change."

> Kerry: "The families think we're here to care for them even when they're here. They do. I had a gentleman I was seeing one evening and I went up into the flat and the family were in and somebody was in the kitchen making drinks. I said: 'Oh, you are making a drink are you? I'll just get this'. No, they were doing *their* drinks, they weren't doing...."

> Gwen: "Their Mum's or Dad's."

> Kerry: " ... because we were going in to do that."

Despite these differing perceptions, it was our observation over the three years that families and friends were in fact around and about in the village quite a lot. Children and grandchildren were often encountered during the times we spent there, especially after school and during the holiday periods. At the time of the second community conference, residents also spoke in very positive terms about the mutual benefits of having and maintaining contacts with younger generations:

> Petra: "We've got a very good relationship with the school but I wouldn't mind seeing the schoolchildren come in more often.... This is one of the things that's coming out now, isn't it: where you get young schoolchildren to relate to retired people so that they're learning from the retired person's experience and the retired person is also benefiting from the youngsters."

> Ben: "When this place first opened the school was sending youngsters up at lunchtime weren't they?"

> Emma: "Yes. That worked well, didn't it?"

> Facilitator: "Do you all share that view because sometimes when we talk to groups like yourselves

people say, 'No thank you. I don't really want to see younger children, I'm quite happy actually'."

> Ben: "I like to hear children."

> Bernice: "Oh, I like to hear them. That's the only thing that I miss, not hearing any children playing."

Encouraging intergenerational relationships, alongside the continued involvement of family and friends in the life of the village, was valuable not least because families can be a vital resource and ally. Consequently, making expectations explicit and having clear channels of communication are important if misunderstandings are to be avoided and the involvement of family and friends is to be maximised.

Democratic decision making

As we have seen, fashioning a new lifestyle is about being open to new opportunities while, at the same time, maintaining some of the links and continuities with one's former networks and activities. As well as being active agents in their own leisure, residents had other more formal mechanisms through which they could contribute their views about village life. These included suggestion boxes (buzz words), the village newspaper and, most importantly, the monthly street meetings.

The various means of involvement in democratic decision making, and particularly the street meetings, are one area of village life that has undergone notable changes over the three years of the study. At the start (in 2000), it was evident that far from being a vehicle for the taking of democratic decisions about village life, the street meetings were poorly attended and not being utilised for the benefit of residents. Originally, up to 18 flats were invited to each meeting. Residents had to come down to the library and the meetings lasted for up to an hour. As a result of observations by the research team and discussions we held with residents and staff (in participation groups and Liaison Meetings), most of the street meetings now take place in smaller groups on the actual streets, with one 'catch-all' meeting held in the village hall. The meetings are shorter, averaging about 20 minutes, and written minutes are distributed to residents. One consequence of these changes is that attendance has more than doubled from an average of about 45 per day to 90-100. As one resident said:

"Everybody comes out now", while another commented that: "More people can say what they think can't they? If you're in a big one, there's just certain people but when you're in your street everybody has to have a say in it more or less, don't they?".

More generally, early on in the study, residents tended to feel that they did not have many opportunities to contribute to how Berryhill was run and managed. At the time of the first community conference (November 2001), the village had been somewhat in the doldrums: the first few years' honeymoon period was over; there had been changes in the senior management team and a difficult period for residents and staff alike over rent increases and amenity charges. This was reflected during the participation groups and at the first community conference, where residents discussed their concerns about how decisions were made and how best to challenge, if necessary, what was happening. Many desired greater involvement, were aware that they needed some kind of forum but felt that the then management of the village were not particularly sympathetic:

Kate: " ... so that there's somebody aware of what's going on, somebody that's got a check on rises, rent rises and amenity charge rises, because otherwise you feel as though they go up and they go up and they go up, and you've got no control over it.... I think that residents should have a say in what's going on.... We don't want everything to be run for us, do we?"

Maura: "No, no, we want a say in things...."

Kate: " ... I think really the residents should have a voice."

All: "Yes...."

Patricia: "Well, I don't quite know how to put it. They [the staff] don't want anyone rocking the boat about, as if they're all happy as it is."

Kate: "Because they want people to think that we're all happy and contented and we don't need to complain about anything. I think that's the whole idea."

By the time of the second community conference (November 2002), the atmosphere was rather different: a putative Residents' Association had virtually disappeared through lack of support but the debate and discussion it generated had stimulated many residents to become more outspoken and expressive. They had also come to recognise that speaking out and influencing the democratic process was not simply about complaining, but about being prepared to acknowledge when things were done well:

Facilitator: " ... if you're happy with how it's run, when would you tell staff that?"

Ben: "I think they find out that if we don't complain then we're pleased about it. The staff will know if we're complaining. So if we're not complaining we must be happy about it...."

Kathleen: "I think if they've got any complaints they'll certainly moan about it and the staff will know...."

Ben: "If people are satisfied very often they don't show it in the same way, but they show it when they're not ... we're not so happy to say when things are done well."

Importantly, these changes were acknowledged and welcomed by staff when they were formally interviewed towards the end of the study:

Maureen: "I think because we have unlocked this talent ... residents are more challenging. It's not a difficult thing but it keeps you on your toes. They're more likely to question now than they did before. They're not as accepting."

Gwen: "They expect more...."

Emma: "I think it's right what Gwen said, they do expect more of you now, whereas earlier on, you know...."

Sylvie: "They were sort of a bit wary of you when they first came...."

Emma: "They jump on you now if it's not done straight away."

Sylvie: "Now they are more willing to speak to you and say, 'We need that doing'."

Liz: "Earlier on it was more, 'I'm sorry to trouble you'.... Those that moved in first that have been here five years now, somehow their expectations from staff and the village are more. Now it's...."

Gwen: "'Why hasn't it been done?', and, 'I've been waiting a week'. They push, yes they push."

Issues about democratic participation and involvement are clearly key to the creation of the new kind of lifestyle for older people espoused by retirement communities. Alongside all the activities and facilities they provide, this is one of the things that distinguishes them most markedly from other forms of institutional living and from the rather restricted lives many people seemed to have lived before they moved in. We return to the wider implications of these findings in the concluding chapter of the report.

Who participates?

When we examined the interview transcripts and our observational data alongside the questionnaires, it was evident that not all residents participate to the same extent in the life of the village. Summarising these findings, key determinants of participation seemed to relate to whether one was:

- *single or part of a couple:* being part of a couple could be helpful in terms of companionship during activities but, conversely, it could also impose restrictions on what one took part in;
- *male or female:* gender differences in participation are often linked with different roles, responsibilities and expectations over the life course and, in particular, there was a sense that the men had retired and "just want to sit back", while the women were more willing and able to join in and mix;
- *a widow or widower:* similarly, while many widowed women seemed to participate extensively in the life of the village, it was a different story for the widowed men;
- *in receipt of support services or not:* a lot of people in receipt of support are brought downstairs in the morning by staff, and amassed together in the village hall or lounge for morning coffee and particular activities. On the surface, therefore, they are participating. In discussion, however, there were some noted difficulties over just how far people could or could not participate and what it

might mean if one member of a couple was receiving support but the other was not. Conversely, those on support were not necessarily the ones who did not want to take part in activities. It was more an attitude of mind – both on the part of the individual and on the part of other residents and staff – that seemed to determine whether or not people would involve themselves, as this resident observed:

Doug: "Some people seem to think that because you're in a wheelchair, you've gone up there, you know, and you haven't. A lot of people are very active up in their mind. Because the body doesn't work it doesn't mean to say that your mind's not working. But that's what you get, I've noticed that. They can be very hurtful at times can't they?... Being 'wheelchair friendly' doesn't mean what it says. It's not all for the buildings, a lot more people need to be wheelchair friendly as well, I think. It needs some education, I think."

Furthermore, as we will see in Chapter 3, just because a resident needed to use a wheelchair did not automatically equate with their being in receipt of support.

Benefits and disincentives to participation

Patently then, a retirement village lifestyle potentially offers older people a great number of opportunities for continued involvement and stimulating activity and company in later life. Conversely, there are certain attitudinal and physical obstacles that may prevent some people becoming engaged in village life to the full. Many of these have impacts on health, identity and well-being, and are discussed more fully in Chapters 3 and 4. Here, we simply note the range of benefits and disincentives that have emerged from the study.

Benefits

The study shows that participation and involvement was important in terms of:

- *the challenge of new activities and opportunities:* which people may either not have tried before, or are able to take up again;

- *giving structure to one's existence:* so that days are not endlessly the same. This is a benefit that the women in particular seemed to stress with many planning their lives around forthcoming activities and trips out;
- *enjoyment:* was a persistent thread in the discussions about activity and suggests that the hedonistic aspects of participation are important and valued by residents;
- *feeling useful and being of help to others:* was particularly important for those who volunteered or who acted as ambassadors;
- *coping better:* taking part in village life and having the support of friends and staff, meant that residents felt that they were able to cope better with, for example, dealing with the loss of a loved one;
- *improved self-esteem and self-confidence:* above all, many residents spoke about how participating in village life had boosted their confidence and made them feel much better.

Disincentives

Conversely, it is not surprising, given the size of Berryhill, the wide age range of residents and the fact that the village caters for a diverse clientele in terms of (dis)abilities and health status (see Chapter 3), that a number of actual and potential obstacles to participation and involvement were identified. These included:

- *poor physical and mental health:* for some people, there were difficulties associated with hearing and sight problems as well as those related to mobility and frailty, and real or perceived mental health problems;
- *design issues:* for deaf residents, the acoustics were sometimes very difficult while those with poor sight could also be left out of things. The open plan design of the village hall, restaurant and bar area was often mentioned as a difficulty and sometimes, residents could not get access to rooms they felt entitled to use like the library and quiet room because they were either locked or being used for other purposes;
- *cliques/monopolising facilities and/or activities:* as in any environment of this size, groups and subgroups formed and, intentionally or not, they could well exclude other residents. Some concerns were raised about people monopolising particular

facilities or trying to impose their views on others and this could mean people felt left out;
- *loneliness and lack of friends:* in an environment with an emphasis on activity and sociability, those without friends (less than 10% over the three years) to help and support them sometimes felt unable to participate. Similarly, those who described themselves as lonely reported less involvement;
- *costs:* for very small numbers of people, the costs involved in taking part (a lot of the activities levy a cost even if it is only a pound) could be a disincentive.

Encouraging and facilitating participation and involvement

Despite the identifiable benefits to well-being that participation and involvement can bring, this sometimes sat uncomfortably with the ethos that one can join in or not as one pleases. This ethos permeates the organisation and, while residents themselves often articulated it, many of them were also acutely aware of the tension between realising this 'choice' while, at the same time, trying to encourage the image of an *actively* ageing community:

> Patricia: "I think it's very helpful to have a lot of other people so you can join in anything if you want. If you do want privacy you've got your own flat there, haven't you...."

> Facilitator: "Right."

> Margaret: "You can take part in anything that goes on in the village but you've also got a choice of what you want to take part in, if it is only sitting down talking to people or joining in any of the groups. You are not forced to go in them but if you want to you can. If you want to go in all the groups, you can join all the groups."

These tensions were also remarked on by external stakeholders, as illustrated by a member of one of the hospital social work teams:

> "The expectation of some people is that they are going to go into an environment where it is literally going to be one big happy family. Obviously that is not going to happen ... I think that with the village,

you are going to get almost a kind of a microcosm of the wider community – some people will want to develop a wide social network and want to get to know as many people and be involved in as many things as they can. Other people may only want to perhaps develop a closer relationship with one or two other people, and there are going to be perhaps people who see themselves as part of a clique ... so, you can encourage people ... but it just depends on what level people feel they want to participate and who with and in what."

At times, however, it is possible to lose sight of just how difficult it is, and how much hard work is entailed in continuously having to encourage and motivate people to participate. Existing residents of Berryhill felt they had a clear responsibility in all this, as Alice explained:

"New people coming in: when they first come in, they don't know what they can do. It's up to us to let them know what things there are available."

Some external stakeholders, like this nurse, also thought it was reasonable for a certain amount of pressure to be brought to bear as a way of encouraging participation:

"I think they [the staff] only pressurise them if they feel it would benefit them, you know, to try and encourage them to. I mean, sometimes I go along and give them a bit of pressure as well 'cos I feel it would benefit. And sometimes, once they try it, they are all right aren't they? It is just they would rather dig their heels in when they've been used to being on their own for so long."

But residents like Doug were adamant that they did not feel pressurised, however subtly:

"I don't think that's true, not here. If you want to take part, you can do, it should be, you know, but there is no pressure on them. They are not up there with a whip saying, 'Get down there or else', you know."

What seemed to be more pertinent was the sense that this kind of environment and this new lifestyle might be better suited to some personalities than others:

Margaret: "Some people want to join in and some people don't, even in here."

Kate: "If you make friends, you do join in more.... And it does give you some incentive to ... or a bit of competition as well."

Alice: "I think it's just their own personality."

Beth: "But then again, if they were living in a bungalow for years on their own, then they are used to their own company. Then they feel that everyone else is intruding.... Which is wrong really. If only they'd get to know that they are better in company. But, it's trying to get through isn't it?"

Kathleen: "I think it's too much trouble for some of them to be honest. I really do, I think they get in their flat and they get comfy and then they don't want...."

Maura: "They don't want to come out."

An ability and willingness to mix and participate was also something that external stakeholder groups commented on. One waiting-list group felt this was particularly important:

Len: "I think you've got to be the sort of person that will mix. Obviously it was made for people to mix ... [but] a lot of people don't. They shut their door and they ignore everybody else, and that's ridiculous to me. They've got everything there: they've got dancing, they've got keep fit...."

Deborah: "Yes, they've got a lot of things going."

Edna: "Yes, I know, that's why I wanted to go."

Moreover, many residents themselves were pleased and proud of the fact that they now had so much going on in their lives:

Alice: "My youngest daughter rings up and says, 'When can I make an appointment see my mother?' [laugh]."

Celia: "Well it's true, yes, we do seem to be getting busier."

Kate: "I mean, I'd love to go to the art class on a Monday and I'd like to go to the sewing class and bingo on a Tuesday and all those sorts of things, but we're out so much."

Alice: "I haven't got time! I've got less time now than I had when I was working full-time...."

Bernard: "Oh I think you get a lot of things in here."

All: "You do."

Celia: "The only way I am going out of here is in a box."

Bernard: "I told them that when I came in, and I tell you something else...."

Celia: "Even if I won the lottery I wouldn't leave here...."

Beth: "No, I wouldn't."

Bernard: "No, I wouldn't. You know, when I come in, I said I shall come out in a box."

Conclusion

Clearly, opportunities for participation and involvement were key to enhancing well-being and developing a new retirement village lifestyle. The facilities and activities available in Berryhill encouraged this, emphasised an active and participative way of life and were much appreciated by those who used them. Being able to volunteer and participate in democratic decision-making forums was also vital to the life of the village. What was especially notable was that Berryhill offered a mix of opportunities that included active and passive pursuits; on-site and off-site activities; traditional pursuits (such as bingo and dancing) as well as more innovative and challenging ones (such as keeping fit, computing and adventure holidays).

Alongside this, peer help, family support and encouraging and maintaining intergenerational links was particularly important, given that many residents had moved from within the local area and were not very mobile. While participation and involvement clearly bring benefits to well-being, not everyone was equally involved in village life. Individual circumstances, together with certain design and attitudinal barriers could adversely affect participation. In addition, distinct tensions emerged around the exercise of individual choice over whether to participate or not, versus the desire to

develop a community with an *actively* ageing identity and ethos.

The challenges here relate to how the diverse needs of residents are met, how involvement is facilitated, and what kinds of links it is important to maintain with the outside world. Account needs to be taken of people's histories, personalities and expectations and there is still difficult and sensitive work to be done to widen participation in the life of the village. It also seems important for the boundaries between the village and the outside world to be as permeable as possible, and for the involvement of family and friends as well as professional groups to be encouraged and welcomed. These kinds of challenges require staff with certain attitudes and with particular skills and aptitudes (in individual and group motivation and facilitation). It also involves a considerable investment of staff time beyond the instrumental, task-oriented activities of their daily jobs.

Summary

- The vast majority of residents were highly satisfied with their flat, the village and its amenities.
- Residents appreciated being able to take part in activities in Berryhill. For women in particular, and for people who need staff support to attend activities, the safety and security offered by having them on site were particularly valued.
- Keeping fit was rated as the most important activity overall; volunteering plays a large part in the life of the village; and organised trips out were very popular and much appreciated.
- For many people, intergenerational relationships with family and friends were maintained and family visit regularly.
- Opportunities for participation and involvement in democratic decision making improved over the course of the study.
- There were clear benefits to taking part and getting involved in village life including being able to cope better and improved self-esteem and self-confidence.
- Some health, design and attitudinal obstacles to participation existed for some people, and participation also varied according to whether or not a person was single or part of a couple; male or female; a widow or a widower; in receipt of support services or not.

3

Health and well-being

Introduction

Health and well-being are fundamental to living a life
of quality in old age. In this chapter we look at how
living in Berryhill affects these key dimensions of
growing older. We do this by drawing on both the
qualitative and the quantitative data from the study in
order to explore:

- understanding health and well-being;
- the health and well-being of residents;
- quality of life and life satisfaction;
- poor health but a better life?;
- maintaining health and well-being;
- meeting diverse health needs;
- health, support and well-being in the future.

We explore too changes over time across all three
waves of the questionnaires to residents, as well as the
views of the various stakeholder groups who took
part in the study.

Understanding health and well-being

In this study, we have deliberately tried to move away
from the traditional definition of health as simply an
absence of disease or illness. Instead, we have been
guided by the now more accepted and holistic
definitions of health and, particularly by Antonovsky's
(1984, 1987, 1996) notion of a health continuum,
along which people of any age can be placed. This
way of looking at health moves us away from a focus
on sickness and emphasises people's own evaluations
of their life circumstances and their sense of well-
being (Bernard, 2000). Most importantly, this
approach takes account of the ongoing relationship

between individuals and their environment, including
their personal relationships, and the social networks
and structures within which they live. As such it
offers insights into how people adapt to changes in
the life course, and how they negotiate both the
losses and the gains inherent in the ageing process
(Baltes and Baltes, 1993; Westerhof et al, 2001).

Like health, well-being is a difficult concept to define
but here, we relate it to quality of life. Traditionally,
too, quality of life has been defined as the degree of
absence of ill-health (Bowling et al, 1997). However,
viewing well-being in this way takes no account of
people's coping strategies or ability to adapt to
change in pursuit of their life goals. Research has
shown that older people tend to closely associate four
things with well-being: their health and functioning;
the existence of relationships and social support (both
of which are considered in this chapter); their
material circumstances (see Chapter 1); and their
opportunities for personal growth and development
(see Chapters 2 and 4) (Steverink et al, 2001;
Westerhof et al, 2001). These factors seem central, we
would suggest, to the aims of retirement
communities. Recently, too, it has been argued that
while the first three of these factors influence quality
of life, it is the fourth which embodies quality of life
itself (Hyde et al, 2003). Accordingly, the importance
of health and relationships, for example, is that they
allow the individual opportunities to satisfy his or her
needs, and it is by exploring the degree to which
such needs are being met that we can most closely
understand a person's quality of life.

At this stage, it is important to note that Berryhill
Retirement Village is located in an area which, in
2000-01 (when we started the study), was classified
among the worst 15% nationally on the Multiple

Deprivation Rank (North Stoke Primary Care Trust, 2003). This in turn has enormous implications for the life expectancy, disease rates and overall health and well-being of residents. Average life expectancy for men and women locally is currently 73.2 and 78.1 respectively, compared with 75.2 and 80.1 nationally (Trinder, 2003).

The health and well-being of residents

Berryhill residents placed great importance on health and, as we saw in Chapter 1, the majority cited current concerns about their own or their partner's health as a major factor in their decision to move to the village. Only two women gave "planning for future health needs" as a reason for moving in. Here, at the first community conference, Reg explains how his wife's health had necessitated their move:

> "She was in hospital before she came here and they said then if we wanted to be together this was the only place to be. So we came here."

Helping professionals also saw ill-health as a major reason for moving in, as one doctor noted:

> "If you're independent and you're healthy, most elderly people seem to really like to stay in their houses and don't want to move there."

These views were shared by other external groups such as residents in a nearby sheltered housing complex, who appeared to view the village as somewhere to go when one could no longer manage:

> "To me it looks, you know, hospitalised, more hospitalised, do you know what I mean?"

Other local residents voiced the opinion that people would only choose to live in Berryhill at a particular age and only then if they had healthcare needs, as Freddie notes:

> "I'd say about 65, and even then only if they're not able-bodied."

Table 3.1: Prevalence of LLI in Berryhill Retirement Village and the local community

Age/ gender	Local community				The village			
	LLI		No LLI		LLI		No LLI	
	n	(%)	n	(%)	n	(%)	n	(%)
55-64	254	(44)	317	(56)	9	(100)	0	(0)
65-74	258	(60)	175	(40)	31	(86)	5	(14)
75+	159	(69)	72	(31)	48	(91)	5	(9)
Male	303	(54)	257	(46)	20	(83)	4	(17)
Female	368	(55)	307	(45)	68	(92)	6	(8)

Limiting long-standing illness

Limiting long-standing illness (LLI) is considered to be a very useful indicator of health status and is widely used in health research. This category of illness includes respiratory, circulatory and musculo-skeletal disorders such as heart disease, diabetes, asthma, emphysema and arthritis. Nearly three quarters of all the men and women living in the village at the beginning of the study reported an LLI (115; 72%). Furthermore, 13 men (43%) and 10 women (17%) lived with a partner who had an LLI. The area in which the village is situated has a 10% higher incidence of LLI than the national average (48% for those aged 50 and over, compared to 38.5% nationally: ONS, 2001). As we can see from Table 3.1 above, the proportions of individuals with an LLI in each age/gender category are higher in Berryhill than in the surrounding community (Jordan et al, 2000), and may well reflect residents' reasons for moving into the village in the first place.

The self-reported incidence of LLI among the core group did not change over the time of the study.

Perceptions of health

We used standardised measures to explore particular aspects of health and well-being. The Short Form-12 (SF-12) rates people's own perceptions of their health and scores are calculated on a scale from 0 (worst possible health) to 100 (best possible health). It is also possible to calculate two different scores, one for physical health (the physical component summary or PCS) and one for mental health (the mental component summary or MCS). Interestingly, it would seem that those with LLI in Berryhill have markedly better physical function than those with LLI in the outside community. By contrast, there is no clearly discernible difference in the mental function scores (Table 3.2).

Table 3.2: LLI and perceptions of health: local community compared with Berryhill Retirement Village

Gender		Age band	Local community		The village	
			SF-12 PCS	SF-12 MCS	SF-12 PCS	SF-12 MCS
Male	LLI	55-64	28.58	49.28	–	–
		65-74	28.60	50.12	39.35 (n=10)	45.28 (n=10)
		75+	23.03	44.72	38.39 (n=7)	46.49 (n=7)
	No LLI	55-64	48.75	53.91	–	–
		65-74	48.20	54.02	–	–
		75+	45.60	54.27	–	–
Female	LLI	55-64	25.44	49.28	37.67 (n=6)	39.92 (n=6)
		65-74	28.28	49.50	36.99 (n=21)	43.50 (n=21)
		75+	18.59	44.17	35.41 (n=41)	45.05 (n=41)
	No LLI	55-64	47.42	53.10	–	–
		65-74	45.26	53.22	–	–
		75+	42.10	53.09	–	–

Note: Figures are means. PCS = physical component summary; MCS = mental component summary. No figures have been given for categories where the frequencies are too small to allow meaningful interpretation.

Table 3.3: Perceptions of health: Berryhill compared with the local community

Age band	The village			Local community		
	n	SF-12 PCS	SF-12 MCS	n	SF-12 PCS	SF-12 MCS
65-74	37	39.72 (7.8)	43.02 (8.4)	1950	39.45 (12.1)	50.16 (10.9)
75+	50	36.86 (6.9)	45.30 (7.0)	1483	34.76 (11.1)	47.31 (11.4)

Note: Figures are means (standard deviations). PCS = physical component summary; MCS = mental component summary.

In Table 3.3, we also compare the local community with the village irrespective of LLI (Thomas et al, 2003).

In the 65-74 age group, the MCS scores are significantly lower in the village than in the surrounding community. The other differences are not significant. This would seem to suggest that the younger residents at Berryhill are markedly less healthy, mentally, than their community counterparts. Taken together with the qualitative data, it would seem possible that reduced mental health (whether through bereavement, social isolation or health issues) may be a contributory factor in the decision by younger residents to move to the village. Additionally, there were no differences in SF-12 scores between those receiving support and those not. Together, these findings suggest that, in terms of mental health particularly, people in Berryhill are not especially well for their age with all the concomitant implications this might have for their sense of identity and for their abilities to take part in village life (see Chapters 2 and 4).

Researchers have also noted that there are significant differences on scores on the SF-36 (of which the SF-12 is a shortened version) between manual and non-manual workers, with manual workers scoring lower (that is reporting poorer health) than non-manual workers, and women scoring lower than men. In addition, people with LLI also tend to score lower than those without such a condition (Jenkinson et al, 1999). Our results then, from a population with both high rates of LLI and a majority of both men and women who were manual workers, are perhaps not surprising.

Loneliness

Loneliness has been suggested as a key determinant in defining well-being and quality of life and at Wave 1 approximately one in five people said they felt lonely (17; 20%). This compares very closely with other studies that show that the proportions of older people who say they are lonely varies between 17% and 30% (Victor et al, 2000). The majority of those who said they were lonely in Berryhill were women (14 out of the 17). By the end of the study, fewer people overall said they were lonely (14; 14%) and there were no significant changes in the findings for the core group. Nonetheless, there were a number of individuals who reported a change in feelings of loneliness. For some, this represented a decrease in loneliness over the period and this is reflected in the qualitative data where people talk about the time it takes to make friends and to feel as though they belong. Esther describes this process at the first community conference:

> "Well, when I first came here I was very lonely, I didn't want to know, I hated the place. I didn't know anybody and everybody had friends of their own and I felt as if I was out of place. Then I felt a bit better and I started to come down here a bit and talk to one or two people but I'm still not settled."

Although there were no statistically significant associations, loneliness featured more among people who lived alone (15; 26%) rather than with another person (two; 8%); for those receiving support (seven; 29% versus 10; 18% not on support); and for those with an LLI (16; 23% versus one; 7% no LLI). Beyond this, it is important to bear in mind that loneliness can be a part of normal existence, particularly when one loses a partner, as Bernice pointed out:

> "We're all lonely at times. Even if you're in your own house or even in here, you can be lonely."

Having someone to confide in was considered important by the majority of both men and women, and most people said they had someone to confide in. There was no difference in this between those on support and those who were not. People also spoke of a change in their feelings of loneliness since moving into the village. Here Milly, a participant at the first conference, contrasts her life now with what it was like before moving in, highlighting the relationship between well-being and loneliness and describing the importance of the support she receives from fellow residents:

> "Yes, I lived in a two-bedroomed house on my own, very lonely. But here I feel a lot better.... It is nice to know that there is someone there that if you need someone, there is someone there for you. You haven't got to 'phone somebody. They are only a few doors away from your home. 'Are you going out?' 'Can you do this?' 'Can you call up there? Go to the chemist for me?' You haven't got to go outside. Just knock on the door. You haven't got to go out in the cold, out in the wet."

In addition, residents acknowledged the importance of the relationship between well-being and health, which Lucy defined in this way:

> "It's about keeping yourself mentally alert: so that you are taking in everything that is going on. You are still living in the here and now and not in the past. You've always got a point of view to pass on. You don't sit back as you're getting older."

Gender differences

Some differences between men and women around perceptions of health and well-being emerged, particularly through the qualitative data. These appeared to be linked to gender differences in ways of coping and adjustment over the life span, as Lil described at the first conference:

> "Both my husband and I within the last four years, we have more or less had two big major operations each and we both had cancer. He had throat cancer, I had bowel cancer. But my daughter will say: 'He's done very well' only because, she will tell everybody, that I've looked after him. I've had to look after him and myself, do you know what I mean? I think if he'd have been left on his own, healthwise he would not have been the man he is now ... he has put his weight back on. So really I don't think he would, men wouldn't look after themselves healthwise like perhaps women would."

Another participant, Freda, also felt that men took a different approach to their health:

> "Well I think women are more inclined to do something about it if they've got something wrong with them than the men do, unless they're pushed into it, perhaps."

Quality of life and life satisfaction

In the questionnaires to residents, we used two standard measures to assess people's quality of life and life satisfaction: the CASP-19 scale and the Diener Satisfaction with Life Scale (SWLS). As was noted in Chapter 1, the CASP-19 measures four domains: Control; Autonomy; Self-realisation and Pleasure (Hyde et al, 2003). Scores range from 0 (purportedly indicating total absence of quality of life) through to 57 (indicating total satisfaction on all four domains).

The mean score for respondents at Wave 2 was 38.0 and there were no differences between men and women or between those receiving support and those not. Comparing this score with some preliminary results from a community sample (Hyde et al, 2003) suggests that residents at Berryhill have a slightly lower quality of life than their community peers across the country (residents' score = 38.0 [s.d. 9.1]; community sample = 42.2 [standard deviation 7.84]). However, the community sample were younger (65-75), and this in itself may account for the difference. At Berryhill, scores were maintained between Wave 2 and Wave 3 and we found no differences in scores between the youngest third and the oldest third of residents in the village.

Once the scores had been standardised for the number of items in each domain, mean scores on the autonomy and pleasure domains were significantly higher than those on the control and self-realisation domains. Moreover, the mean pleasure domain score was significantly higher than the autonomy domain score. This would seem to suggest that freedom from unwanted interference from others, and especially pleasure, contribute most to residents' quality of life.

The Diener Satisfaction with Life Scale (SWLS) measures subjective global life satisfaction (Diener et al, 1985). It has five questions and scores range from 5 (low satisfaction) to 35 (high satisfaction). Again, we found no gender differences or differences according to whether or not people were receiving support, and the scores were similar across all three waves of the study. The average score on this scale for Berryhill residents was 24.62 which compares very closely with a wider community score of 25.8 (Diener et al, 1985).

Poor health but a better life?

On the face of it then, it seems that Berryhill residents suffer considerable levels of poor health, particularly in relation to the prevalence of LLI and the mental health status of younger residents. They also have slightly lower quality of life than their counterparts in the wider community. By way of contrast, however, our results also show that those with LLI function better physically in the village than those living out in the wider community.

We also asked people what their life was like since moving to Berryhill and how it had changed in the past year. Figure 3.1 shows that, at Wave 1, just over half of the 54 people in the core group (28; 51%) indicated that life was "much better" since moving to the village. At Waves 2 and 3 this plateaus, with a majority of respondents then indicating that life is "about the same" as it was a year previously. Initially, moving to the village is clearly seen as a change for the better after which most residents seem to remain reasonably positive. For small proportions, however, life worsens. This pattern was similar for both men and women.

Those respondents surveyed at all three waves (the core group) were also remarkably consistent in their assessment of their health, claiming that it did not change from year to year. Qualitatively, too, residents like Petra, a participant at the second community conference, noted that:

"With this environment, people seem to feel better than other people that are living out in the community."

Maintaining health and well-being

Residents spoke positively about the opportunities for health maintenance and about the support available within the village. They also highlighted the well-being service and nutritional issues when considering health maintenance strategies.

Help and support

At the beginning of the study, 45 of the 159 residents (28%) were receiving support services from the organisation. At Wave 2, this had gone up to 34% and at Wave 3 it was 31%. As noted in Chapter 1, residents received support at one of four different levels. The highest percentage of people were receiving Level 2.

We asked residents if they felt able to afford support but, at Wave 2, 41 people (43%) declined to answer this question. A third said they could afford it (31; 32%) while the remainder said that they could not (26; 27%). When exploring the issue of the support needs of residents, it is important to take into account that almost three quarters of respondents (65; 71%) said that their family was their most important helper, with 14 residents (15%) saying it was staff, and eight people (9%) mentioning friend(s) in the village. The results from Wave 2 also suggest that a high

Figure 3.1: Life since moving to Berryhill Retirement Village (core group Wave 1; Wave 2; Wave 3)

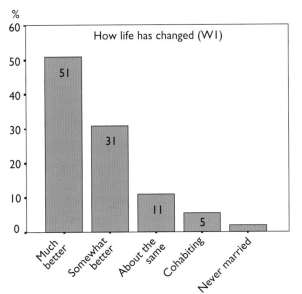

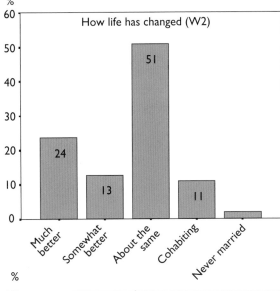

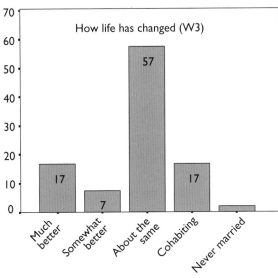

percentage of those receiving support from staff lived alone (31; 96%). One factor that may go some way to explaining this is that, on average, those people living with someone were significantly younger (70.9 years) than those living alone (76.3 years).

When we examined these data more closely we found some interesting gender differences. While the majority of both men and women relied on family as their main source of support, this was more prevalent among the women (53; 76% compared with 2 = 57% men). Conversely, higher percentages of men than women reported relying on friends in the village (three [14%] compared with five [7%]) and on staff (five [24%] compared with nine [13%]). It would seem from this that the majority of participants in the study looked to their family as their main source of help. This has important implications for intergenerational relationships (see Chapter 4) but also contains within it important distinctions, for example between what could be expected from friends – social support – and what staff could be asked to do – physical care. Two female residents at the first conference summed this up in these terms:

"I would get the staff to come, not trouble friends."

"You wouldn't expect them (friends) to come in and wash up for you – keep it friends."

On the whole, residents were very positive about the support available in Berryhill, giving it an average satisfaction score of nine out of ten. Alice, who received Level 2 support, felt there was a big improvement in her life since moving to the village from a nursing home. Nonetheless, she made the important observation that, no matter how good the support might be, there was an almost inevitable indignity in requiring someone else to provide intimate personal care:

"Oh yes, but here the caring staff make it so much easier. It's very good. It is so much easier but the indignity is still there."

For other residents like Mary who were not receiving support packages, there was still a sense of being supported:

"As I say, I've always found that you can talk to them [the staff]. If there is something that you are not happy about you can talk to them, just ask their advice: what about this? What should I do about this?"

Other residents also pointed out the differences between help in the wider community and that available in the village. Here is Georgina at the second community conference describing her experiences:

"When I had falls in my other house, I used to have a lifeline. They had to shout and come in over the intercom to ask you if you were bleeding first. Then they had to ring my daughter, and she can't drive now because of her back. She had to get her husband off work to come up and see to me. But if you're bleeding, like I did cut my head open once, the ambulance will come first, or else you're lying there, sort of thing. When I fell in here, they were there in a few minutes. It's sort of different."

Such differences around support had significant implications for family as well, as these two respondents to the family/friends questionnaire noted:

"When my parents were able to move into the village we as a family were extremely grateful: it gave them safety, care and peace of mind."

"I'm extremely grateful for the care/quality of life my parents have received since moving to the village and count them as fortunate to have a home there."

The well-being service

Three years after Berryhill Retirement Village opened, it was decided to appoint a well-being advisor. There was concern to move away from the notion that this would be a nursing service, because of a desire to emphasise well-being rather than disease. However, with a nurse employed, the post became known among residents as the well-being nurse. Residents who used the service, which predominantly focuses on well-being checks (for example, blood pressure monitoring, dietary and exercise advice), were very satisfied, describing it as "very thorough", and giving it an average satisfaction score of nine out of ten. They felt it offered the security of knowing that health issues might be picked up early, before they could become problems.

GPs and other health professionals also saw the service as offering an important improvement in communication and liaison between themselves and the staff of the village, as one local GP explained:

"We used to get a lot of requests for visits, but at the carer's request: the patient didn't even seem to know we were coming, or know why ... we'd get there and I'd say: 'Well, why am I here?'. And they'd say: 'I don't know, why you're here? And that's much, much less since the nurse has come in because I think s/he's filtering a lot of that."

Another GP also remarked on this:

"It does, for me, depend very much on management structures, and the nurse has been an asset and has sifted out stuff for us, so that we don't get called to [rubbish], with little information and unnecessary...."

Yet, some external healthcare professionals saw the level of support offered by the service as being very basic and there were some concerns that it was creating more work. For example, if existing health issues were being monitored by the GP (for example, blood sugar levels, blood pressure), occasionally patients would return for unplanned consultations because of worries generated by their contact with the well-being service.

Nutrition

Obesity, coronary heart disease and cancers are all significantly higher locally than nationally (North Stoke Primary Care Trust, 2003), and are high risk factors for premature death. Nutrition is an obvious key factor in each of these, and is closely linked to quality of life in older adults (Amarantos et al, 2001; Drewnowski and Evans, 2001). In the first year of the study, catering standards were not considered by residents to be very good. When the subject of the restaurant came up in discussions, residents voiced their discontent about the food, which seemed predominantly high fat, low fibre, overcooked and with low proportions of fresh fruit and vegetables. As a respondent to the family/friends questionnaire also noted:

"The food on offer needs to be better prepared and presented. Sometimes meals are cold when served or swamped in gravy."

During the time of the study, changes were made in the standard of food available and it became more obvious from observation that account was being taken of various dietary requirements, for example of people with diabetes. This was particularly important because one out of three residents using the restaurant were in receipt of support services. This improvement was reflected in a slight increase in the satisfaction scores that residents gave for the restaurant between Waves 2 and 3 (8.3 and 8.5 respectively). Furthermore, at Wave 2 the lowest score given was one out of ten, while at Wave 3 the lowest score was six.

The role of professionals

A wide variety of social and healthcare professionals have contact with Berryhill. These include both acute and long-term social workers, community psychiatric nurses, district nurses, occupational therapists, physiotherapists, opticians, chiropodists, health visitors and GPs. In interview, they told us that they saw developments like Berryhill as an additional accommodation and care option that would suit certain older people, but not necessarily everyone. Some of these groups held regular surgeries in the village, for example the chiropodists and the opticians. However, while happy to provide home visits should the patient's condition require it, GPs were very resistant to the idea of a surgery in the village itself:

> "I think that if you said to us that the demand on us to go and visit the village was going to increase over [time], because of institutional reasons rather than ... because individuals can't get to the practice, that wouldn't fit in with my view of how primary care is going to be delivered over the next few years. Or I think the government's view of how primary care is going to be delivered."

Interestingly, this view was shared by many residents who, at the second conference, spoke about how important going out to a GP of one's choice was because it fostered independence and maintained a relationship that had been built up over a long time:

> Annie: "Well, you've got to go on your own steam as long as you can, haven't you?"

Facilitator: "Do you see that as important in terms of the things we were talking about this morning about maintaining your health?"

Bea: "It's still keeping some independence, isn't it?"

Daphne: "Oh yes, I believe in that. If I can do it myself, I do."

Meeting diverse health needs

All groups who took part in the study (residents, staff, family and friends, health and social care professionals) voiced some concerns about the suitability of the environment for those with particular health needs. Here, we look at terminology and attitudes, physical disabilities, mental health needs, and death and bereavement.

Terminology and attitudes

We have already mentioned in Chapter 1 the confusions that were present around some of the terms used on an everyday level in the village. An important example of this, which is closely linked to perceptions of ageing and health, is the language used about the services designed to meet the health and support needs of residents. In the official brochures, the reference is to 'support' but both staff and residents consistently referred to the formal help from staff as 'care'. Indeed, as we have previously noted, staff employed as Resident Support Workers were consistently referred to as 'carers' by residents and regularly referred to themselves as such. Requiring 'care' from the staff appears to connote need and dependency, rather than indicating supported independence. For certain residents then, this seems to be at variance with the ethos of 'active retirement', leading to possible tensions. One of the male residents at the first conference highlighted this when he indicated that for him, 'going on care' was about others doing for him what he could no longer do for himself:

> "I keep wondering when I will go on care: when I can't manage. I shall go on care when I can't manage shopping and bathing, you know."

Another resident at the same conference highlighted the negative perceptions around between requiring support and sustaining the village as a retirement community:

"There are far more that are on care and it seems that it is getting more a nursing home."

Such statements and concerns were common in the various public meetings attended by the researchers, and were voiced regardless of whether or not any resident receiving support was present. It was also apparent that some people associated physical aids, such as wheelchairs, with supported residents regardless of whether or not this was in fact the case. Moreover, such attitudes seemed to be exacerbated by the visibility of those with disabilities, particularly in the mornings in the communal lounge, compared to the relative invisibility of highly independent residents who spent significant periods of time out of the village.

A further example was the tendency of a number of residents to assume that frailty was the domain of older residents. Such use of language may strike others as alienating and discriminatory. It also raises concerns over the effects such attitudes may have on the well-being of disabled residents within the village community.

Physical disabilities

At Wave 2, over half of respondents had sight problems (51; 52%) and over a third had hearing problems (38; 39%). Here, Margaret notes the difficulties faced by fellow residents who have sensory impairments:

"There's one lady I know that's blind and deaf so she can't come. Well there's two of them: neither of them can join in. But they would love to, you know. Edith would like to play bingo for a start. Mary is – she can't communicate unless it's one to one because she can't hear because of background noise – she can't join in much at all."

Other physical health problems, particularly those associated with mobility, could work against independence and participation. Tilly described how her disability increased her sense of isolation, which seemed only to be emphasised by her reliance on staff:

"The only people I've seen since I've been here is the cleaners ... nobody knows. I am living on my own most of the time because I can't walk. Physically it is my balance. You see I'm not safe now because I lose

my balance. So I am more or less tied to my flat.... I do [come to the street meetings] but I have to be fetched and taken down."

In some cases, it could also mean withdrawing from community life as Ellie, another resident, noted:

"You see, I don't come down so often as I did [before hip replacement]. It is too much effort to walk."

The physical layout of the building could also pose a challenge to those like Ellie for whom the size of the building, including some of the communal areas, meant it could be difficult to interact with others. Some residents found the distance from their flats to the lifts difficult while, for those in wheelchairs, the weight of the doors, both to individual flats and along the corridors, could be problematic. Here Alice highlights her dependency on the help of others:

"Well my sister does a lot for me but I've got very good neighbours and they keep an eye out for me. So if I am having a struggle getting into my flat, getting the door open and they are coming by, they will say: 'I will do that for you'."

Mental health needs

Another area of concern was around meeting the needs of people with mental health problems. From discussions with healthcare professionals it appears that dementia type illnesses, and anxiety and depression, were the most common mental health disorders among their patients in the village. Professionals felt that where patients had complex conditions, typically involving both mental health issues and physical dependency, then they "did not do so well". The size of the building, and the similarity in layout along the various corridors, could exacerbate any tendency to be disorientated and further confuse people, leading to increased isolation. In particular, it was noted, that any tendency for a client to 'wander' because of a dementia type illness was not sustainable within the village, not least because other residents and staff found it difficult to cope with.

Many of the healthcare professionals who were interviewed considered that these kinds of patients would benefit from smaller, perhaps sheltered, housing environments with more structured day care.

They were also concerned that residents on high levels of care (funded by social services) were not eligible to attend local day care facilities that might be better tailored to their individual needs:

"And they would have benefited from a more structured day care as well. So, if they were in the community and they were in a sheltered bungalow, say for instance, then they could attend a day centre or some form of structured place where they would have got mental and physical stimulation. In the village, although they have got like the keep-fit and they have got certain activity sessions that they do, they don't always fit into that. And because they're in the village, if they aren't able to pay for these extra services because they're on a high level of care, they're not eligible then to go to a day centre or whatever."

Furthermore, they felt that mental health problems were not identified at an early enough stage by the staff of the village, that interventions tended to happen at crisis point, and that residents would receive more quality time with community-based carers:

"I don't know how they work out their rotas but it seems very difficult for the people who I've been visiting ... they don't know who half these people are who come in [to their flat] ... it's just that they come in and they might say, 'Morning Mrs ... ', whatever her name is, but they won't say who they are. So they're in and they're out and they [resident] haven't got a clue who they've seen."

For those residents with mental health problems of a less complex nature, such as anxiety or depression, the size of the building, the number of residents and the consequent prevalence of cliques could also be a problem. New residents reported being told "you can't sit in that chair, it's so and so's". This kind of attitude might be uncomfortable to any new resident, but for those with particular sensitivities it could be extremely alienating and further deepen their anxiety or depression.

Berryhill staff were themselves very aware of issues around meeting the mental health needs of residents, but recognised that they were not especially well equipped or trained to meet these needs. Here, one member of staff describes her colleagues:

"They don't know how to deal with people with mental health problems. They don't know how to talk to them. Their whole attitude is wrong."

Staff too felt that the size of the building could be problematic because as Maureen noted:

"I think as well that the environment doesn't lend itself to supporting people with mental health problems, particularly because the building is so big. Sometimes they can be so far away that it's hard to support somebody if you're not there, or within easy reach of them – and that's a problem."

Concerns about meeting the mental and physical health needs of residents were further deepened by apparent confusion over the training and qualifications of staff in the village, with one resident at the first conference, for example, insisting that: "Lorna [staff member] is not a carer, she is a trained nurse and a trained midwife". In fact, although very experienced as a carer, Lorna was neither of these. Residents also voiced concerns about too few staff being available within the village to support those with particular needs.

Death and bereavement

The need to address issues around death and bereavement emerged as another important challenge. Five (6%) of those responding to the Wave 1 questionnaire had died by the time of Wave 2. Between Waves 2 and 3 a further 10 (10%) respondents died. In Berryhill as a whole, over the period of the questionnaires (January 2001–June 2003), 13 men and 24 women died. The majority of family and friends mentioned residents dying, and the possible effects on the well-being of remaining residents, as a major disadvantage of this type of age-segregated living environment. Residents too voiced concerns, as these two participants at the first conference explain:

Margaret: "You see the problem here is when somebody dies in here we all know. Now, if we lived in a street or round the block as we used to call it, you wouldn't notice it so much. But, when you get used to people in here and you know who they are, and they die, you just know and that's it ... we expect people to die, everybody has got to die...."

Kathleen: "And when you live outside, there isn't just old people is there, there's young ones and everyone, so it doesn't seem as bad. But, when you're in here well, we're old aren't we, you know what I mean?"

Throughout the study, residents spoke of death in ways that seemed to suggest it had a prominent, although often veiled, place in the village. Some coped with this issue through a process of distancing: death was something what happened to 'others' and which happened everywhere, as Patricia illustrates:

"You felt terrible in here when they first started dying. I used to think, ooh, you know? You do care when you've been in here so long, and people outside used to say: 'There's another man died in the village, isn't there?', or 'There's another lady died, there was one last week'. So people outside were counting up the people who were dying in here. But I said, well, they are all elderly people, they're all pensioners, they would have died anyway if they'd have lived out in the community, wouldn't they?"

However, some residents did acknowledge the effects of grief, both on themselves and on the village community as a whole. During the second conference, Petra observed:

"You get a lowering of the morale in the village when this happens, particularly with two or three people [dying around the same time]. Particularly with the people that they've been close to, those that have been in longer, that came in with them. The atmosphere changes ... following a death in the village."

They also identified particular benefits to being in the village at times of bereavement, as these two residents explained during the second conference:

Maura: "Much more [support] than I would have got if I'd have lived on my own [outside]. I don't think I could have coped on my own. But because I was in here, and I had got Kathleen next door to me who came into me every day, and loads of other people, I had a lot of support."

Kathleen: "And I think also when it happens to you, you know what it's like, don't you? You know what other people are going through, if it happens to you."

Thus, while residents appeared to feel that one coped with bereavement better because of the presence of so many peers at Berryhill, at the same time there was a sense that the concentration of older people in one place could bring its own intensity.

Staff, both in the questionnaires and in interview, identified counselling skills and bereavement as areas in which they would appreciate further training. Through discussions with the research team, steps were taken to deal more openly with issues around death and bereavement and the manager was put in touch with an experienced bereavement counsellor. She was invited in to explore ways in which the staff and the structures of the village might respond more positively to residents' needs. One tangible result was that an anniversary book was established which commemorates those who have died.

Health, support and well-being in the future

Concerns about their future health needs were of importance to many people. At Wave 2, about half of those asked said they thought their health would deteriorate, with half saying they did not know what to expect. Little difference was found between men and women although the women were slightly more positive about their future health than the men.

In addition, we broke the question down into physical health and mental health. As Figure 3.2 shows, the majority of people said they expected their physical health to get worse (47; 52%), with few expecting it not to do so (nine; 9%). However, only 16 people (17%) expected their mental health to get worse. Thus, large proportions of people were uncertain about their future health. This was more evident with mental health expectations, where the majority of respondents said that they did not know (54; 60%), than in relation to physical health expectations (35; 38%). It is difficult to know whether this response represents a real uncertainty as to future health prospects, or a reluctance to engage in a consideration of issues connected to ageing, as highlighted in the earlier discussion around coping strategies connected with death and bereavement.

Support in the future was another key issue for residents. Nine out of ten people said that they were confident that more help would be available at

Figure 3.2: Responses to the statement "I expect my physical/mental health to get worse" (Wave 2)

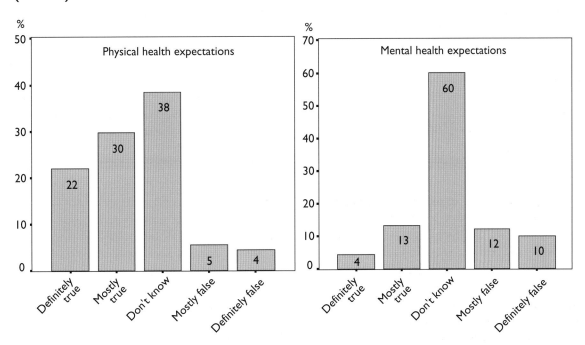

Berryhill should they need it. However, it is interesting to note that when people were asked if they could see circumstances that might affect the suitability of the village as their home in the future, one in five said yes. These concerns centred entirely on health, and were primarily linked with worries about shortages of staff and quality of care. For some people, there was a sense too that this might not in fact be a home for life, and that they would have to move on. Here, Mary, a resident with sight problems, voices these concerns:

"Up to now, I mean I am so far fine, but with my sight gone ... I would have to go in a residential home, if my sight went. I'm comfortable at the moment, but just how far it will go I don't know. But I'd rather be here than there as things are. I'd rather be here than there in any case."

Others wondered about the potential for becoming isolated in one's own flat and being solely dependent on staff for support, contrasting Berryhill with what they saw as some of the more positive features of nursing homes:

Brenda: "I don't want to be shut away. I don't want to be taken up when I can't, you know. I don't want to wait for them to bring me down and come for me. I feel that I want something different because I went into Silverton, the nursing home

there. My sister's mother-in-law is in there and I thought the set-up was ideal. She's in a small ward with about four beds with their own wash-hand basin. She could see what was going on and a hand was there if she wanted to go back to her bed. She wasn't shut away. They'd got a lot more facilities like bathrooms and all that, whereas here, the carers are a bit limited, aren't they really, with the washing?"

Janet: "That's what I feel, because I've been in a lot of places and what is the point of me having a kitchen if I can't use the cooker? And things like that. Or a bathroom that I can't use, just to be pushed into my living room and then them [staff] come and take me out or put me to bed."

Conclusion

Berryhill clearly offers a variety of opportunities for support and socialisation, both of which contribute to an improved sense of health and well-being for the majority of people. This is especially important given that the population the village serves has a significantly low health status when compared with national norms, and health issues were the most important reason for moving in. However, for a small number of residents, particularly those with more significant or complex physical and/or mental health needs, the environment of the village may itself exacerbate their condition and potentially lead to increased isolation. Indeed, loneliness featured more for people with health needs requiring support from the organisation, and there were some concerns about the ways in which less confident newcomers are enabled to feel welcome in the community. In addition, the physical layout of the building can facilitate or hinder the independence of those with disabilities.

A number of challenges arise from this, most notably in terms of how best to meet the diverse health needs of residents. These include the importance of addressing terminology and attitudes, questions about the suitability of the environment for people with complex physical and/or mental health needs, and dealing with death and bereavement.

Beyond this, it was also evident that staff were generally considered to be very supportive and helpful. Nonetheless, participants across the study (for example residents, staff themselves, health and social care professionals) identified a number of key training areas in relation to the health and well-being of residents. These included supporting residents and staff in bereavement, basic group work skills and communication skills. More particularly, there appeared to be gaps in staff skills when it came to supporting those with more complex physical and/or mental health needs.

Summary

- The area in which Berryhill is located, and from which almost all of the residents have moved, is rated below the national average on key indicators of health and well-being.
- Health issues were very important for residents and the majority of respondents cited current concerns about their own or their partner's health, as the main reason for moving to the village. This view was shared by a variety of stakeholder groups, including healthcare professionals and local residents.
- Three out of four residents suffered from an LLI, and this was higher than one would have expected to find in the outside community. However, respondents with LLI in Berryhill have better physical functioning than their peers with LLI in the community.

- Scores on the SF-12 showed that respondents had somewhat lower mental health functioning than their community counterparts, but the same, or better, physical health status. Levels of functioning were maintained over the three years, and there were no differences between men and women, or those on support or not.
- Loneliness featured more for those who lived alone, for women more than men, for those receiving support, and those with an LLI.
- Respondents recorded similar (Diener) or lower (CASP) quality-of-life scores in comparison with others of a similar age living in the community. Pleasure, and freedom from the unwanted interference of others, were the factors which contributed most to quality of life.
- Although their health status may have been poor, substantial proportions of respondents felt that life had got much better since moving to Berryhill, and this was maintained over time.
- Residents spoke positively about the opportunities for health maintenance within the village which, in addition to involvement and participation in activities, included help and support from staff, the well-being service and support from professionals.
- About one third of residents were in receipt of support and this remained stable over time. Support was rated very highly although there were some concerns over its affordability both now and in the future.
- Family remained the most important source of help for the majority of people, and for women in particular. Proportionately more men relied on staff or friends.
- Future health and support needs were of importance to many people although most were uncertain about what precisely those needs might be. More respondents expected their physical, rather than their mental, health to get worse. While nine out of ten people were confident that general help would be available if they needed it, one in five were worried that, for health reasons in particular, the village might not in fact be a home for life.

4

Growing older: age and identity

Introduction

Retirement villages like Berryhill are distinctive places in which to live. This is reflected in the fact that everyone who lives there has to be over the age of 55. Although there is no upper age limit, such communities are defined largely by age and age differences with respect to other groups. They can also be contrasted with negative aspects of life in local neighbourhoods, particularly where these are seen as threatening or dangerous environments for older people to live in. They are also distinguished from residential and nursing home environments where independence is perceived to be under threat and 'old fashioned' notions of dependency and decline are still seen to hold sway (Biggs et al, 1999). By contrast, retirement communities are intended, in theory at least, to take the best from both worlds and to be environments that enhance both security and autonomy for older people.

What, therefore, is it actually like to live and grow older in such a new environment? Drawing on qualitative and quantitative data from various phases of the study, this chapter considers this question by exploring:

- understanding age and identity;
- experiences of age and identity;
- intergenerational relationships;
- perceptions of others;
- reasons for living in Berryhill retirement village.

The chapter concludes with a look at some of the challenges facing such communities: challenges that are developed further in the final chapter of this report.

Understanding age and identity

We think we know what age is: it is the time passed, in years, between birth and how old one is now. But age can also be something that is felt, experienced and is reflected in appearances. How one thinks about one's age can depend on a variety of factors, such as the environment one lives in, perceived health status and the attitudes of other people (Moody, 1986). Each affects how age is perceived and how it is responded to. In other words, the effects of chronological age depend on identity: how individuals think and feel about themselves and their own ageing.

Rather than dealing with the material facts of a situation, the study of age and identity focuses on how people interpret their world. The question asked is not so much whether A is in good health for their age, but rather what do they think, feel and do about their health? Thus it is possible to find older people who appear to an outsider to be frail and unwell, but who report that they feel good about themselves, and maybe even better than they did when they were younger (Biggs, 1999a). Consequently, if identity addresses the way that we experience ourselves, it can be expected to have a significant effect on our sense of confidence and satisfaction with the rest of the world. It exists at the crossroads of our psychological and social selves. It is affected by our physical and mental state and how others respond to what they see.

The possibility of maintaining a positive identity in later life is a complex one because, as we age, the relationship between our bodily health, our psychological well-being and our social environment becomes increasingly interdependent (Baltes and

Carstensen, 1996). As we have seen earlier in the report, older people's sense of confidence can be closely related to their physical health and can be dependent on finding a supportive environment that helps compensate for disabilities. Mental health too may depend as much on a good social environment as on physical support. For example, we saw in Chapter 2 that an important element of the 'stay active – stay young' philosophy espoused by Berryhill is the opportunities it provides for continued learning and achievement, plus a sense of shared decision making and participation. In Chapter 3, we further discovered that, despite widespread health problems, many people in fact feel that their life is much better in the village than where they lived previously, and that they are able to maintain a level of functioning and well-being because they are in a supported and supportive environment. In other words, the village aims to create an environment that, in Glenda Laws' terms (1995, 1997), supplies positive social and spatial 'props' to an ageing identity.

Experiences of age and identity

According to this viewpoint, retirement communities that provide these kinds of social and spatial props can, in turn, be launch pads for the development of a new sort of identity with which to grow old, as participants at the first community conference highlight:

Facilitator: "Do you think you are growing older in a different sort of way because of living in the village?"

Maggie: "Yes I do."

Facilitator: "Oh, have you?"

Maggie: "More happy in a way I would say, yes."

Hannah: "Yes, you are."

Maggie: "And secure."

Sue: "There is a lot to do, isn't there?"

Hannah: "If you want to do it, isn't there?"

Maggie: "You don't have to sit in your flat if you don't want to do, do you?"

Sue: "And life is more interesting here, isn't it?"

The reports of older residents also indicate that with ageing, what you see is not always what you get. Just as an objective measure of health may be an inadequate gauge of a person's subjective sense of well-being, so physical appearance may be a poor indicator of the inner life of the older adult, as this planning group for the first community conference discussed:

Alice: "But it doesn't always relate to age, does it? When you say 'an old person', there's persons with an old mind that stay in a groove."

Maura: "You can be old in years, but not.... "

Kathleen: "Not in mind, yes."

Kate: " ... you know, it isn't until you sit down and talk to somebody that you realise there's a lot going on behind that quiet little thing that's sitting in a wheelchair. You just don't realise just how much is going on. They remember interesting things that they've done and that sort of thing."

Alice: "I mean, if you accept being ... you don't want to read, you're not interested in politics, you're not interested in this or that and you, you just age. You just age. But if you want to do things, and try to do things, you're staying young."

Kathleen: "I don't think of myself as old, you know. When I go to anybody, go anywhere and tell anybody about old people, and what I think and do, I say, 'Oh, I'm old myself'. And I don't really, I don't really."

Growing older, feeling younger?

In the questionnaires we addressed different ways of thinking about age and identity. Residents reported their chronological (or actual) age, said how old they felt inside, thought they appeared to others, and how old they would like to be. Comparing actual and 'felt' age gives a numerical indication of the disparity between how old people feel inside and how old they are in years. Thus a number of questions that are relatively easy to administer and to understand help us to unpick how people think and feel about their own ageing. First, we looked at how people compared their actual age with how old they felt inside. With respect to their actual age, 62 (84%) of the 74 people who responded to this question felt younger or the same age inside and 12 (16%) people said they felt older (Figure 4.1).

Figure 4.1: 'Age felt inside' compared with actual age (Wave 1)

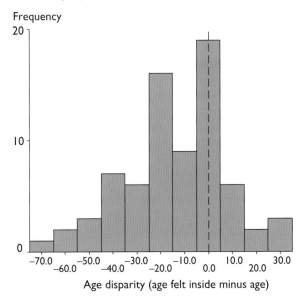

Note: The dashed vertical line indicates equivalence of actual age and 'age felt inside' (a disparity of zero). Mean = – 13.70.

Figure 4.2: 'Age would like to be' compared with actual age (Wave 1)

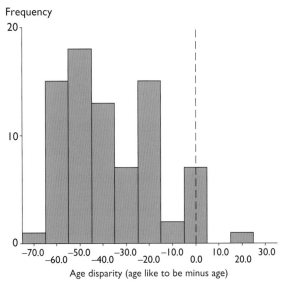

Note: The dashed vertical line indicates equivalence of actual age and 'age would like to be' (a disparity of zero). Mean = –37.10.

Figure 4.3: 'Age seen to be' compared with actual age (Wave 1)

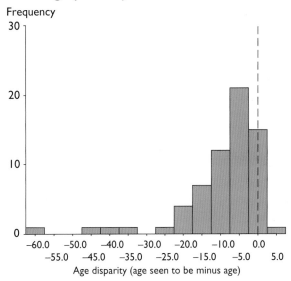

Note: The dashed vertical line indicates equivalence of actual age and 'age seen to be' (a disparity of zero). Median = –6.00.

The disparity scores were then compared with self-reported physical and mental health as recorded by the SF-12. They were also compared with well-being and other aspects of identity such as gender in order to 'map' the different dimensions of age and identity that exist in the village. Second, we compared people's actual age with how old they would like to be. With the exception of one respondent, everybody wanted to be younger than, or the same as, their actual age (Figure 4.2).

Finally, in Figure 4.3 we can see how old people thought they looked to others in comparison with their actual age. Here, only two people reported that they thought they looked older than they actually were.

In other words, the majority of people who responded to these questions generally felt younger, thought they looked younger and wanted to be younger than their actual age. Age and identity was measured in these ways at the beginning and at the end of the study and we found that these attitudes were stable over time.

At the end of the study, these disparity scores were also compared with the physical and mental health components of the SF-12, with the Diener Satisfaction with Life Scale and with the CASP scale (Table 4.1). Focusing on the statistically significant correlations, these scores indicate that the greater the difference between one's actual, or chronological, age and the age one feels inside, the higher one's mental health score and the higher one's quality of life. Similarly, the greater the difference between one's actual age and the age others see one to be, the greater one's satisfaction with life. This suggests that the more people felt and saw themselves as younger, the better their overall sense of personal well-being. None of the disparity scores seem to be related to physical health; what associations exist are with psychological aspects of well-being.

When the pattern of correlations in Table 4.1 is considered as a whole (ignoring their magnitude and whether or not they are statistically significant), two noteworthy points emerge. First, feeling younger inside, or believing that one is seen as considerably younger than one is (that is large differences on the disparities involving 'age felt inside' and 'age seen to be'), appears to be 'good', as these are associated with higher scores on the various measures of well-being. In contrast, a large difference on the 'age like to be' disparity seems to be 'bad', as this is associated with low scores on the measures of well-being. So, if there are large differences between how you feel inside and your actual age, and between how you think you look to others and your actual age, this is perceived positively. However, if you would like to be a different age to how old you are, chronologically, this appears to have a negative influence. In other words,

feeling a younger age inside and actually wanting to be younger have opposite effects.

Feeling older

We also took a closer look at the 12 people in Berryhill who said that they felt older than their actual age. As Table 4.2 shows, this phenomenon appeared to be closely related to their scores on the physical and mental components of the SF-12: our measure of health status. Those who felt older than their actual age had a significantly lower score on the physical component than those who felt younger, and a slightly lower (but non-significant) score on the mental component.

These 12 people were also less likely than those with negative or zero disparity scores to agree that their health was excellent and, in the future, they expected it to get worse. This same group were significantly more likely to report low life satisfaction as measured by the Diener scale. In other words, people who felt older inside than they actually were had poorer perceptions of their own physical health and lower general satisfaction with their lives. Poor health may therefore go some way to explain why this group of people felt older than their actual age would suggest.

Table 4.1: Age identity, health status and life satisfaction (Wave 3)

	'Age felt inside' minus actual age	'Age like to be' minus actual age	'Age seen to be' minus actual age
PCS	−0.101 (*p*=0.390)	0.112 (*p*=0.346)	−0.005 (*p*=0.972)
MCS	−0.320 (*p*=0.005)	0.052 (*p*=0.663)	−0.139 (*p*=0.304)
Diener SWLS	−0.187 (*p*=0.093)	0.231 (*p*=0.039)	−0.349 (*p*=0.004)
CASP	−0.370 (*p*=0.002)	0.218 (*p*=0.072)	−0.259 (*p*=0.058)

Note: PCS = physical component summary; MCS = mental component summary. Correlations based on *n* between 54 and 82. *p*<0.01 was taken as the cut-off for statistical significance, in view of the number of correlations performed.

Table 4.2: 'Age felt inside' disparities compared with health status

		PCS		MCS	
Score	*n*	Mean	Difference	Mean	Difference
>0	10	28.10	8.28 (*p*=0.034)	43.24	7.93 (*p*=0.142)
≤0	55	36.38		51.17	

Note: PCS = physical component summary; MCS = mental component summary. Two of the 12 respondents with positive disparity scores had missing values on the SF-12.

Maintaining a positive age identity

Surprisingly, there were no differences between men and women on the age and identity questions. Neither did scores vary as residents' time in Berryhill grew longer. This may indicate that the village attracts a certain type of person with these attitudes to later life. It may also indicate, as we suggested earlier, that the sort of environment they are living in helps in some way to maintain these attitudes. Alternatively, these responses may reflect a general view of ageing held by many older adults but, because there are no comparative data from other groups of older people, it is currently not possible to say which of these alternatives is the most likely. However, when these quantitative findings are set alongside some of the observations made by residents in the qualitative elements of the study they suggest to us that the village environment is a key factor in helping older people maintain a positive age identity. Residents' attitudes correspond with an ethos that accentuates a positive ageing environment although this active involvement is tempered somewhat by the widely held view that the real secret of a good old age is to live in physical, psychological and social comfort. This is what Berryhill supplies, as this conversation among participants at the first community conference illustrates:

Ann: "Live comfortably here."

Melanie: "A comfortable life and have friends and no worries."

Ann: "Nothing to worry about."

Grace: "We've worried all our life, haven't we, now it is our turn, do you know what I mean, what I'm getting at?"

Ann: "It is our turn."

Melanie: "So it is our turn now at our age."

Facilitator: "So is the meaning of life to be comfortable?"

Melanie: "Of course it is."

Grace: "Oh yes."

Age identity, ageing bodies and peer support

That retirement communities are defined by age gives issues of identity a particular twist and living with people of approximately the same age group, and coping with the challenges of an ageing body, are two of the important tasks facing Berryhill's residents.

The company of peers

The company of peers was an issue discussed in the small groups at the first community conference:

Hazel: "I think you've all got the same views on life when you are older, more in the older age group, you've all got more or less the same views on life, haven't you, I think?"

Maura: "Much more than I would have got if I'd have lived on my own. I don't think I could have coped on my own. But because I was in here and I had got Kathleen next door to me who came into me every day, and loads of other people, I had a lot of support."

Hazel: "Yes, that's one of the joys of being in here, when you don't see as much of your family but then you've got people your own age, you've got the company."

While peer company is important in maintaining a positive identity and high levels of peer interaction characterise retirement communities, reliance on age peers for support can come under stress as individuals get older and their needs increase while their capacity to help others decreases. In this study, we did not find an emphasis among Berryhill residents on peer support as a factor that characterises the whole community, in contrast to our previous study of a smaller community (Biggs et al, 1999). Rather, specific friendship groups were identified as supplying companionship and direct support in times of illness and incapacity. As we have seen in earlier chapters, there was also a clear distinction between neighbourly concern and respect for people's privacy, and an expectation that friendship should not replace family support or the help from staff or other professional groups. Sometimes, however, these boundaries could become overstretched, as Margaret explains:

"On odd occasions I've brought Madge down, but I cannot take her back up, because she needs help. I took her up once, which I was told was alright, and I had problems putting her on the loo and then I had to pull the cord and fetch someone to her, 'cause I don't want that responsibility. But I mean, if they're in the wheelchair, I mean, I can push her down – there's not much of her, you know, she's light as a feather – but I couldn't push anyone about, if they were heavy or anything."

Living with an ageing body

Linked with this is the inevitable need for people to manage their ageing bodies, as Kate noted in one of the planning groups for the first community conference:

"I mean, an elderly, disabled person, because I mean when you're past a certain age you've got something wrong with you, haven't you? Arthritis or something. I mean, sometimes, it's nice to be in a safe area."

This was something others too were aware of and was discussed during the first conference:

Esther: "I mean you must admit we are living a lot longer now than we've ever done."

Moira: "Within your limitations."

Agnes: "Yes you can please yourself and you know if you are poorly or ill you've only got to pull the cord and so what can you do? If you were in a house and you were ill, you would perhaps sit there for days wouldn't you?"

Angela: "My health has been better since I've been in here because I haven't got the worry of being on my own if I'm ill and who is going to find me."

Rachel: "Because you don't know what you are going to be like, even the next day. You've got to do things while you can and while you've got the energy."

Moira: "Yes, do things today."

Moreover, as we also saw in Chapter 3, whatever one's circumstances, maintaining good health is key to a positive ageing identity.

Age and generations

Another important aspect of growing older in retirement communities concerns the link between different ages and generations. Chapter 1 showed that Berryhill caters for a wide range of people from the age of 55 to more than 90 years. This can be a strength, but it can also lead to tensions within the community.

Generations within the village

Older residents at the first conference tended to think that generational differences were minimised by living in the village:

Judith: "I am sixty-four but I never feel this generation gap at all. Some people are old, old and some people will never be old, it is the way they think."

Rachel: "I think with age, you can have younger ones fifty-five and I think it would even out maybe."

Judith: "Yes."

Gerry: "The generation gap decreases in here."

Judith: "I mean but look at Mabel upstairs, she talks just the same as us and she is fifty-five, but she talks just like us at our age you know."

This was also echoed in another discussion during the same conference:

Alice: "I've been in here two years and … until he had a birthday a few months we were on a level, he had a party and it was his sixty-fifth birthday. I'm old enough to be his mother! But when you're together, you're the same age."

Maura: " … and then sort of coming to live in a complex where you're all sort of one big family, or you've got your own, you can all be together or you've got your own."

Younger residents were, however, more conscious of some of the differences and problems that can arise:

Doug: "We were on about the dancing. They said, 'Why aren't you dancing?' I said, 'Well I don't know what dancing you're doing, because I was in the sixties'. We had the jive and the twist and they're doing ballroom things. I don't know anything about it."

Facilitator: "How do you distinguish between the different generations in here?"

Lydia: "Just open your mouth!"

Doug: "[laugh] That's it, yes, and wait for something to come out.... There are people in here as old as my Mum and Dad."

Beth: "It doesn't make any difference though, does it?"

Nora: "It doesn't make a difference because we're all one big family, aren't we? And as in a family, we're all different generations, aren't we?"

Facilitator: "What sort of difference do you think it makes, then?"

Doug: "They're a different generation; they've got different values than us."

Lydia: "I can't put my hand on it really, music for one thing."

Nora: "Different music, that's the biggest one, the music. You get the young ones, the middle ones and the older ones. The older ones want the old music, the middle ones want middle-of-the-road music and the younger ones want young music."

A second factor that tends to create subgroups within the 'one big family' of the village is its size. When it comes to identity in groups, size matters, as Margaret highlights in one of the planning group discussions:

Facilitator: "Do you think the size of the village affects people's feelings that they can join in?"

Margaret: "No. I don't mean that the village is big in that way but you might find some people in one area and some people in another, and they don't go into the same place as you, so you don't know them or you don't see them if they don't come down into the sitting room. All you'll do is see them going backwards and forwards to the flat."

So, while the age basis of the village holds the advantages of support and understanding from people who are in similar age circumstances, and may allow certain forms of intergenerational relationships to flourish, it also raises problems. The emergence of different generational groups within Berryhill with, for example, different tastes in music, entertainment and other leisure activities, can lead to subgroups emerging that increase the complexity of organisation and coordination, and can lead to tension in the community as a whole.

Intergenerational family relationships

A further aspect of age and generation concerns relationships with family members. We saw in Chapter 2 that residents still maintain strong links with families, but the emotional distance that community living affords may allow family relations to be redefined, and experience shared across generations in ways that it was not possible to do previously. Here, these residents reflect on the growing life experience of their children and on their own increased self-awareness:

Kathleen: "I think your family take more advice off you: your own children themselves take more off you when they're getting older, than they did when they were younger, don't they?"

Alice: "Yes."

Maura: "Yes, they do."

Alice: "Tom will listen to me more now."

Kathleen: "Because they seem to think as they know it all, 'We know it all because we', you know, and they know better than you. But, when they're getting older I think the advice you give them, it kind of sinks in and they know, don't they?"

Maura: "Yes."

Alice: "Yes, and when they have children for themselves."

Kathleen: "Of their own, yes."

Alice: "Jennifer's said to me, 'Mum, I'm just beginning to understand'...."

Kathleen: "I think, when you're getting older, you have got knowledge of things and you can give advice. Sometimes they don't listen and then they say, 'Ought to have listened to you, mum, you were right', and things like that, you know. I think you can't foresee things, but you can: you can foresee things happening, can't you really, in some things?"

The ageing of the community over time

While the mixing of generations within Berryhill can create differences of opinion, there was also considerable concern about the ageing of the community as a whole. This is particularly the case where the activities that residents maintain for themselves need to be kept going by fresh cohorts of retired people coming through. In Chapter 2, we noted some of the anxieties about the difficulty of recruiting volunteers and here Alice articulates these worries during one of the early planning groups:

"Unfortunately, I think we're going to lose the dancing class. There's three more sessions and then they want someone else to take over. Laura and Fred that have been doing it all the time we have been here, Laura isn't very well and she's finding it a bit difficult. So they're going to hand over to somebody else if possible but up to now we haven't got anybody."

In Chapter 3, we also highlighted the impact of death and bereavement in the village. Not surprisingly, a concentration of age peers within the same place makes these kinds of experiences much more visible than if people were living in the wider community, and accentuates how the village is ageing over time. Residents were acutely aware of this:

Kathleen: "They've lost a lot of neighbours: my old neighbours, while I've been in here."

Patricia: "A lot of them would have died wherever they were because they were old and whatever they had got wrong with them they just couldn't get better."

Maura: "You get it more in this sort of environment, don't you, and in our age groups?"

Patricia: "It's because we are all together ... people talk: 'Oh they're all dying off in there'...."

Kathleen: "That's what I say: we're all the same age group. When we are outside there are young ones with families and you don't notice it so much do you as when you're in here?"

The prevalence of illness and death, and the potentially negative effect on the mental well-being of residents, was also highlighted by external stakeholders and by some family and friends in particular. Furthermore, many of the original group of 'pioneer' residents held strong views about the positive and anti-ageist values of the community although it is evident that these belief systems have become diluted with the ageing of the community and with successive waves of residents coming in.

Perceptions of others

Despite this, people who live outside Berryhill but have a stake in it (such as family and professional helpers) were generally supportive of the village. The overall perception of family and friends seemed to be one of a secure and safe environment, as summed up by this respondent who described the village as being: "A safe and pleasant haven for our elders". According to family and friends, another big advantage seemed to be having a social environment in which one could access the company of peers who would share common interests. Again, one family member commented that the village was: "fine if you like to be involved most of the time with other elderly people". Similarly, health and care service facilities also featured as an important advantage.

One consequence of this was that the majority of family and friends who took part in the study remarked on how residents seemed to have a greater sense of self-confidence:

"Since my mother has lived in the village, there has been a change in her in that she's happy and enjoying the company of older people of her age group."

This sentiment was also expressed by a broad spectrum of helping professionals and is encapsulated by one of them who said: "Companionship and confidence are given to all, like a new lease of life".

However, some of the tensions that we have noted as being associated with ageing inside the village are brought into sharp contrast by fears about how the outside world sees it. One concern is how this will affect whether new, younger retirees will be attracted to live at Berryhill. Some residents take an ironic attitude to what are perceived to be the prejudices of the wider community, as Doug pointed out at the first conference:

"They've got a notice there: 'It's this very old retirement village', you know. So they keep away. 'You don't want to go there, it's full of old fogies', you know."

The (mis)perceptions of others were also raised in one of the other discussion groups during the same conference:

Heather: "My sister lives in the heart of the country, miles from anywhere and I get her tights. Well, sometimes when I go up, in between I said to her and she said, 'Oh what will I do about my tights when you go in there?' [laughter]. 'What do you mean?' She said: 'Well how will you be able to get out to get them?' I said: 'Well I'm not going in prison' [laughter]. They don't know. They don't realise what it is like."

Dorothy: "Well, they've got the idea that it is a home you know."

Moira: "You are locked in and you can't get out."

Heather: "They don't realise you are in a self-contained flat."

Moira: "Yes, they don't understand that, do they?"

Dorothy: "A lot of people like ... when you take people round, show people round the village, they can't believe what it is like. It's all right you talking to somebody and telling them you live in a village, [but] they've got see it for themselves, haven't they?"

Margaret: "When the village was first built, people thought, exactly like they thought about Rose House: it was a home. And we must stress on people that it's not a home, it's a village. But I think now, after we've been here for this short time, well, for three years, that people know now that it is a village, a retirement village and not a home."

Even though residents think external people now know and accept that Berryhill is different from other kinds of environments, our interviews with older people living in the local neighbourhood highlighted some of the misunderstandings that persist. Mixed-age local neighbourhood groups saw Berryhill as being exclusively for "old folks", while some members of a nearby sheltered housing development thought that they would not like to live in the village because "there's too much illness in there and that would get me down". Others wondered whether residents had in some way given up on their previous communities and did not believe that the problems of security were as great as some residents maintained. Professional stakeholders, including some staff, echoed this notion of "giving up" and the idea that Berryhill was a place to move to when one could not cope in the community.

The possibility of segregation from the wider community was another concern mentioned by stakeholders. For example, it was felt that the downside of the company of peers might be that residents become cut off from other parts of society. One respondent to the family/friends questionnaire put it this way: "Their association is only with their peer group and this does not reflect the age spectrum of society as a whole". Healthcare professionals too voiced the view that residents moved in with particular expectations that might reinforce an inward-looking culture. Their perception was that, for many residents, "This was their last move and that they were going to be looked after and sorted", while another family member thought that residents saw themselves "As past it – in the final stages of life".

Other issues highlighted by stakeholder groups included concerns about loneliness if residents could not find a way of 'fitting in' with established groups within the village itself. Some family and friends were also worried that, in some cases, the environment had a negative effect and eroded self-confidence and self-esteem if people felt they were unwelcome at activities. Staff in particular highlighted the relative isolation of older men who, they felt, could be "very set in their ways, and can only be encouraged to try new things at a push". On the other hand, they felt that the women were "eager for company".

These generalised perceptions can be contrasted with the important point made by a number of healthcare professionals that it is crucial to take individual personalities and needs into account. In thinking about this, however, concerns were also expressed again about the overall size of Berryhill and its potential effects on individuals:

> "I think going into somewhere large like that can actually be a bit overwhelming for one person on their own unless they've got really good social skills."

Furthermore, external stakeholders wondered about the broader social implications of developing retirement villages and what they say more generally about society's treatment of older people. As one healthcare professional put it:

> "It's a terrible cop-out isn't it? It's like saying we're going to give up: we cannot have you living in your house and be safe. We can't police it. You can't be safe: there'll always be louts so give up and move out and we'll put all the nice people together, and let the rabble out there destroy the estates in peace. It's almost like we've given up."

Despite this, there was widespread agreement between stakeholders that retirement communities like Berryhill would play an increasingly important role for people in later life.

Reasons for living in Berryhill Retirement Village

Having considered these different dimensions of retirement community living from a variety of perspectives, we return to a question with which we began this study and this report: why live in a retirement community like Berryhill? As we noted in the opening chapter, retirement communities are intended to enhance a certain sort of ageing: one that is active, free of age prejudice and positive in its encouragement of certain forms of self-expression. This is reflected in ExtraCare's publicity material, which states:

> "By providing choice and opportunities – things younger generations take for granted – and by encouraging real and meaningful activity, we're promoting health and happiness."

Beyond this, and distilling down the findings from the study, it seems to us that residents themselves gave three main reasons for choosing to live in Berryhill,

Berryhill: Main entrance

Photograph by Stephen W. Ellis

each of which impacts on people's sense of positive identity. The first of these was *autonomy*: the freedom to engage in activities, hold beliefs and express oneself without fear of sanction, so long as this does not impinge on the freedoms of others in the same community. In the case of identity, this means the ability to express age-related interests and concerns, not to be treated as second-class citizens and to have control over one's own personal and private space, as Patricia explained in one of the early planning groups:

> "It's like you've got your own privacy. If you wanted to, you can shut your door and that's your house and you've got your privacy if you want it. If you want a bit of company, like we say, we just come downstairs as opposed to sitting in one another's flats sort of thing. I've never been one for neighbouring like, you know, but I've always been friendly with everyone."

The second reason was *security*: a sense of feeling safe to engage in one's everyday activities without fear or intimidation. In our study, this was often expressed in contrast to the experience of living in the wider neighbourhood outside the village. Crime, vandalism, drug abuse, noise and, in some cases, victimisation were all cited as concerns. More commonly, residents commented on the loneliness and responsibilities of living outside the village, as this small group discussion during the first conference illustrates:

> Gerry: "I feel more relaxed here than I did out there. I've got no pressures in here as I had there. I was worrying about whether the house was big enough to carry on, 'Where are we going to go?' you know; 'What is going to happen to her? Are we going to be split up?', and things like that. But here we won't, so we can get on with living. It has taken a lot of pressure off."

> Sally: "You feel safe at night and that bit of security round the building, because somebody is next to you. You haven't got to run outside or anything, they are next door."

This sense of being secure was echoed by other residents like Kate:

> "When you've lived on your own in a bungalow or in your own house, there's always the fear of being

broken into, kids throwing stones and all sorts of things outside ... [here], you feel secure."

Finally there was *sociability*: the opportunity to socialise with others, and not to be lonely or socially excluded. Residents most frequently expressed this as control over the balance between social interaction and private activity and rest. It is the choice of when to 'go down' to the public community areas of the village and when to spend time in the privacy of one's own flat, as encapsulated in this discussion:

> Dorothy: "All being in this one building but having your own flats, you can come down and talk to one another and can stay there. That's all the difference as opposed to living in your house before where you were just on your own. So it is a different way of life, isn't it?"

> Patricia: "I think if you keep on taking an interest in things and talking to people and mixing, whereas if they live in a house on their own it just stops, doesn't it? They've got no conversation with anybody and they get older and they don't go doing things. So I think this sort of place changes all that, doesn't it? It's mixing with other people and doing things, isn't it?"

These reasons are important in maintaining a positive identity because they hold the promise of being able to be oneself and develop one's potential in a supportive environment. In terms of age identity, this means not having to hide parts of the self for fear of the reactions of younger age groups or age peers with negative attitudes to old age. It also implies an opportunity to share common concerns based on age.

Conclusion

The strong statements made by the publicity for retirement communities appear to have been accepted by many residents at Berryhill. They are goals that are strived for and are reflected in the generally upbeat and positive assessments of village life reflected in our conversations with residents. With respect to age and identity, we have seen that the majority of residents tend to report that their inner selves do not correspond to their outer appearances and that they feel younger inside than their chronological age (Biggs, 1999b). They also associate this with improved mental health and an ability to cope with what are seen as the inevitable physical consequences of the ageing body. However, some caution is advisable in linking these findings exclusively to living in Berryhill. While evidence is sparse, it would appear that older people generally feel happier and more contented than younger adults (Erikson et al, 1986). They are also less likely than other age groups to associate well-being with physical health, even though they suffer from more physical disability and illness (Bernard, 2000). One possibility therefore is that retirement communities like Berryhill may be enhancing this natural capacity to cope with an ageing identity, rather than creating an entirely new experience for older adults.

It is also important to note that the relationships between the different age identities examined here are open to a variety of different interpretations. Does, for example, a big gap between 'actual age' and 'age felt inside' mean that people are more or less satisfied and at ease with their age identity? It could be interpreted as showing that people feel much better about themselves than they expect to at that age (indicating an optimistic scenario in which retirement communities make people feel better about ageing than is generally the case). Alternatively, the same result could be interpreted to mean that people are discontented with who they are because they have such a big difference between their inner feelings and external reality. The findings on mental health and well-being would indicate that, among the group of older people under study, a large disparity is more likely to reflect the former, optimistic situation. On balance then, we would interpret this as evidence supporting the positive effects of living in Berryhill.

Another important influence on the atmosphere and identity of the village has been the ageing of cohorts of residents over time and relations between generations within the village itself. As residents grow older, the overall population of the village becomes older too, unless there is a regular recruitment of residents at the younger end of this age spectrum. Although there have been attempts to attract younger adults that have met with varying degrees of success, some external perceptions of the village also seem to have discouraged people in their fifties from joining. The challenges here concern the image of Berryhill among prospective residents and the need to maintain a balanced community age profile if the present ethos and atmosphere is to be

preserved. Alongside this, in a large community with a multiple generational profile a variety of tastes and lifestyles need to be catered for and this may place tensions on the maintenance of a village-wide identity as subgroups inevitably emerge. A key challenge to Berryhill will be the future management of these trends: the need to maintain the overall age of the community so that it includes both younger and older retirees; the need to adapt to individual ageing without putting off prospective residents; and the need to maintain the overall ethos of autonomy and active lifestyles.

Summary

- A wide variety of interests and activities are used by residents to support their ageing identities. These social and spatial props can be launch pads for the development of a new sort of identity with which to grow old.
- It appears that residents generally felt younger inside, thought they looked younger and wanted to be younger than their chronological age. These attitudes were stable over time.
- The younger residents felt inside compared to their actual age, the higher their levels of mental health and life satisfaction. Similarly, the more residents thought others saw them as younger than their actual age, the greater their life satisfaction.
- Those who felt older than their actual age had poorer physical health status.
- There were no differences in age identity between men and women, or over time. This may indicate that the community attracts a certain type of person with these attitudes to later life.
- Peer support was an important factor in maintaining the spirit of Berryhill but it did not characterise the village as a whole. Rather, specific friendship groups were identified as supplying companionship and direct support in times of illness and incapacity. There was also evidence that reliance on age peers for support can come under stress as individuals age and their needs increase while their capacity to help others decreases.
- Clear distinctions were made between neighbourly concern and respect for people's privacy, and there was an expectation that friendship should not replace family support or the help from staff or other professional groups.
- Common concerns based on age were an important part of residents' identities and the

mixing of different generations of retired people is key to the continuing vitality of Berryhill. Certain forms of intergenerational relationships within and beyond the village also flourished. However, while the age basis of the village holds advantages, it may also cause tensions and lead to the formation of subgroups.

- The emotional distance that community living affords can ease interactions between family generations.

- People who live outside Berryhill but have a stake in it (such as family and professional helpers) were generally supportive of the village, welcoming the opportunities provided by the social environment, the company of peers, the sharing of common interests, and the provision of health and care service facilities.

- Other stakeholder groups held a variety of (mis)perceptions about Berryhill and the people who lived there. The village was variously seen as being exclusively for old people; for those who had "given up"; and as a place to move to when one could no longer cope. Concerns were also expressed about those who did not "fit in" and about the relative isolation of older men.

- Berryhill, like other retirement villages, offered autonomy, security and sociability – all factors that facilitate the development of a positive environment in which to age.

5

Conclusions

Introduction

In this concluding chapter, we first provide a brief overview of the main findings from the study. Although the research lasted for three years, it is important to stress that it is not, and cannot be, a definitive and conclusive piece of work – Berryhill Retirement Village was in existence before the study began, and will continue to evolve and develop long after we have left. In other words, the study provides insights – from one particular time period – about what it is like to live and work in such an environment. That said, there are a number of wider implications of these findings for others who might wish to develop similar forms of accommodation and care for older people in the future. This discussion is therefore organised around five different areas:

- the nature of retirement communities in Britain;
- what's in a name? – terminology and attitudes;
- accommodating diversity;
- staffing such environments;
- links with the outside world.

Given that a key feature of the study was the close involvement of older people as active participants in the research process, the chapter concludes with a brief look at the impact the research has had on those with whom we worked.

Improving the lives of older people

Essentially, this study has enabled us to examine the contribution that one new model of accommodation and care can make to improving the lives of older people. In exploring the wider implications, it is important to remember that Berryhill was located in a deprived urban area that was significantly below the national average on key indicators for health and well-being. The village itself was large compared with more traditional accommodation and catered for, on average, 160-75 residents at any one time. As we saw in Chapter 1, residents were exclusively white, women outnumbered men in a ratio of 2:1 and the majority of residents lived alone, often because they had been widowed. The average age of village residents was between 75 and 76 and, from answers to the questionnaires, it was clear that health-related issues (affecting oneself or one's partner) were the prime reason that people had moved into the village. From our qualitative work, it was also evident that people were anticipating that their health might become an issue for the future. The village had a staff team of 38 people who, between them, were on duty throughout a 24-hour period.

Opportunities for **participation and involvement** were key to developing a new retirement village lifestyle, and the kinds of amenities and activities available in Berryhill facilitated and encouraged this. Chapter 2 showed that the majority of residents were highly satisfied with the facilities and services available to them and, largely because of issues around safety and transport, they appreciated being able to take part in activities on site rather than going out. Volunteering also played a large part in the life of the village, both in the opportunities it provided for individual role and skills development, with concomitant potential for enhanced self-esteem and self-confidence, and in terms of the community itself acting as its own resource. Volunteering extended beyond the residents themselves to the staff, members of the local community, and family and friends. In addition, many residents maintained external relationships with family and friends, and family visited regularly. Certain formal structures within the village, such as the regular street meetings, offered further opportunities for involvement in democratic decision making. However, the study also identified that the ability to participate in village life could vary depending on whether, for example, a person was single or part of a couple; male or female; a widow or widower; in receipt of support services or not. In addition, some health, design and attitudinal barriers to participation existed for some people.

In terms of **health and well-being**, residents in the village suffered with more LLI than their counterparts living in the community and this may well link with their reasons for moving to Berryhill in the first place. However, Chapter 3 revealed that despite being 'unwell', residents generally had better physical functioning than their peers with LLI in the community and they also maintained their health and well-being over the three years of the study. There were no significant differences in health status scores between those receiving support and those not. Residents also spoke positively about the opportunities for health maintenance within the village although such opportunities could be more limited for those with significant physical and/or mental health problems. In particular, loneliness was experienced more by those who lived alone, by women, and by those receiving support. One third of residents received support services from the organisation and this proportion remained stable over the three years of the study. For many residents, family remained the most important source of help. With regard to quality-of-life measures, residents' scores were similar to others of a comparable age but key features of their quality of life were freedom from the unwanted interference of others, and pleasure.

Looking at issues around **age and identity** shows that Berryhill offered residents autonomy, security and sociability, all of which facilitated the development of a positive environment in which to age. It also appears from the findings in Chapter 4 that residents generally felt younger inside, thought they looked younger and wanted to be younger than their actual age. However, those who felt older than their actual age had poorer physical health. In addition, the autonomy that is afforded by living in a retirement community can enhance interaction between different family generations. In exercising their autonomy, and in supporting and developing active identities, residents used a wide variety of

interests and activities. Common concerns based on age were an essential feature of peer support for residents. Such support is an important factor, both in facilitating the individual's development and in maintaining the ethos of the community. Moreover, although the mixing of different generations of retired people is key to the continuing vitality of the community, this may itself lead to tensions.

Implications for future service and policy developments

Having reviewed the findings about Berryhill, we now turn our attention to the wider implications of this study for those who might be considering developing similar retirement villages in the future.

The nature of retirement communities in Britain

First, it seems to us that new retirement communities in Britain contain some, but not necessarily all, of the features of both North American and European developments. British developments, like their American counterparts, lay emphasis on the leisure and activity dimensions. Indeed, despite the use of the word 'retirement' in the titles of many of these developments, they are keen to challenge this concept and to emphasise the importance of participation, involvement and activity as a means to maintain individual health, identity and well-being as well as the wider vitality and dynamism of the community as a whole. Peer support and the retention of intergenerational family relationships are also important dimensions. In other words, the essential nature of British retirement communities seems to us to be about developing, supporting and managing a process of 'optimal ageing', both individually and collectively (Minkler and Fadem, 2002). The results of our study also show that, despite the difficult and impoverished environments and work histories of residents and their concomitant poor health, such villages can work well for working-class older people and, unlike many North American and European communities, do not have to be planned and developed just with middle-class professional retirees in mind.

A few years ago, we defined retirement communities as having:

- a *retirement* element: residents are no longer in full-time employment and this affects their use of time and space;
- a *community* element: an age-specific population, living in the same geographically bounded area;
- a degree of *collectivity:* with which residents identify and which may include shared activities, interests and facilities;
- a sense of *autonomy* with *security* (Phillips et al, 2001).

While these basic features are still helpful in defining such places, what they do not do is characterise them according to the kinds of people who live in them; what their motivations for moving are; how they are situated financially; or what their expectations and hopes are, both for themselves and for the community more generally. From the findings of the current study, what has become evident is that these definitional features are not absolutes. Rather, each element of the definition encompasses a spectrum of circumstances and activities. For example, while these communities may well have a *retirement* element in the strict sense that everyone is retired from paid work, residents of such villages do a whole variety of other forms of 'work' both for themselves and for others. Thus, many of them undertake voluntary work of various kinds, as well as supporting and helping their peers.

Similarly, while these may be age-specific *communities* with everyone aged over 55 and living in the same geographical area, they in fact accommodate a number of different generations. Likewise, the degree of *collectivity* is just that – a matter of degree. Some communities may be very collectively minded, others may well be less so, and this will be affected by things like size, cultural dimensions, financial circumstances, health status, personality factors and so on. Lastly, we found that *autonomy* and *security*, while important defining features, may also mean differing things to different people and be experienced in rather different ways depending on one's individual

Berryhill: Ground floor flats

circumstances. For some people, autonomy might mean having been able to lift the burden of care from family members; for others it might mean the freedom to take part in activities that they have always longed to do but have never been able to. Security too can be felt and experienced differently: retirement communities offer both physical security perhaps away from the fear of being broken into or robbed; but they are also important in terms of psychological and emotional security.

As more and bigger retirement communities are developed, the likelihood is that these definitional features will, in reality, encompass more and more complex dimensions. This in turn is likely to lead to a variety of interest/subgroups within a given community that will all, potentially, be competing for space and resources with each other. We would suggest not only that retirement communities need to articulate very clearly what they are trying to achieve, but also that ways of managing the inevitable tensions in an overtly proactive way (through, for example, mediators or staff with mediation skills) are challenges that will have to be addressed in the future.

What's in a name?

Beyond definitional issues, it has become evident that living and working in a retirement village throws up related concerns around terminology and attitudes. Many communities have, as we noted earlier, 'retirement' in their title. However, we would argue that the word 'retirement' sits uneasily with the kind of active participation ethos that such villages seem to be trying to promote. Far from wanting people to retire or be retiring, these environments are very much about encouraging participation and involvement. They provide opportunities for engagement in a variety of active and passive pursuits, on-site and off-site activities, traditional pursuits (such as bingo and dancing), as well as more innovative and challenging ones (such as keeping fit, computing, adventure holidays and volunteer work). Moreover, the participants in our study pointed out that using the phrase 'retirement community' or 'retirement village' often meant that both they and their families had certain expectations of the place: that people would be 'looked after' as if they were in a retirement home. It can also affect the perceptions of people outside who may well see these communities as places exclusively for (frail) older people. In other

words, they may be seen as places one goes to in order to retire and cut oneself off from the rest of the world.

Closely linked with this are tensions between an ethos of active participation, and the fact that these developments are also offering support of various kinds. This too is reflected in terminology, especially that used to describe staff and available support services. As we saw in Chapter 3, both residents and staff in this study tended to use the word 'care' rather than 'support' to describe the services available. Thus, residents were commonly described as being 'on care'. Again, we would argue that such labelling can carry with it negative connotations of frailty and dependency. Helping professionals can unwittingly reinforce this view. On the one hand, retirement communities can and do provide professionals with another option in terms of the resources they are able to offer older people – and for this reason are often looked on favourably and positively. On the other hand, if professionals have long-term involvements with residents they will be working mostly, by definition, with the frailer and more disabled members of such communities. The danger here is that it could be the negative dimensions that get underlined rather than the more positive ones, as succinctly encapsulated by this helping professional:

"I just wanted to make the point that the danger in interviewing a team of social workers is that you are getting an unbalanced view. There are a lot of people who are very happy and we never see and unfortunately it's only the ones where there are problems that come to light."

Where retirement communities also diversify their activities to bring in and cater for groups with particular health needs such as people with dementia, or those suffering from Parkinson's disease, this too can affect how residents and helping professionals view such places. For residents who might primarily identify themselves as members of an active retirement community, reconciling this with the presence of people who clearly need substantial levels of support from the organisation can be difficult. Again, these are tensions and challenges that we would suggest need further attention from those developing and managing such communities.

Accommodating diversity

Retirement communities like Berryhill commonly cater for people over the age of 55. With a potential age span of 40 years or more, it is therefore difficult to argue, as much North American research has done, that they are age-homogeneous communities. Notwithstanding the fact that residents tend to share the same socioeconomic background, what seems to us to characterise these communities more is the diversity of the people who are attracted to live there and of their needs, in contrast with other more traditional forms of accommodation and care. Indeed, we would further argue that the social policy move in Britain towards promoting these developments as places for 'fit' and 'frail' older people as part of the Supporting People programme (ODPM, 2003) also underplays the complexity.

For developers, policy makers and providers, we would emphasise three particular challenges to accommodating diversity from the work we have undertaken. The first challenge is how retirement communities accommodate different (age) groups and generations. In Berryhill, we saw the emergence of different generational groups with, for instance, different tastes in music, entertainment and other leisure activities. There were also important distinctions according to whether one was single or part of a couple; a man or a woman; widowed; disabled and/or receiving support; lonely and isolated or with many friends and acquaintances. A second challenge concerns the gendered aspects of these communities. From our study, retirement villages like Berryhill seem appropriate environments for meeting the needs of many older women but perhaps do not address older men's needs quite as well. The third challenge relates to the spectrum of 'wellness' that exists among residents and how this is viewed and handled by older people themselves, staff and helping professionals. In other words, it will not be enough for developers of the future to rely on simple and straightforward assessments: they will have to take a more nuanced approach that encompasses people's histories, personalities and expectations when addressing their diverse needs.

Over and above this, there are important considerations about what facilitates or prevents people accessing such places. Economic factors in terms of affordability are crucial, as are health, cultural and social dimensions. How such communities are designed and where they are located will also impact on who is able, or not, to get access, and on the nature and quality of the lives that people lead within them. As individual community members grow older, attracting younger retirees becomes increasingly important. And, as these new retirement communities themselves age over time, accommodating this dynamic diversity presents challenges for the future management of such places. If retirement communities are to remain environments in which to age well, these challenges should not be glossed over: meeting the diverse needs and expectations of older people beyond a basic focus on accommodation and care will be increasingly important.

Staffing retirement communities

This leads on to another set of challenges around staffing retirement communities, particularly in relation to staffing levels, attitudes and skills. While Berryhill may be unusual in having all its staff (except the newest recruits) trained to NVQ Level 2 as a minimum (see Chapter 1), in general, staff in these and similar environments are not especially well qualified or well trained (Cameron and Moss, 2001). Moreover, where there are competing employment opportunities, especially for women, in the retail and service industries, then retirement communities may well face potential difficulties over continuity of staff and what can reasonably be expected of them given their levels of pay.

Beyond the task-oriented activities of the job (how to lift and handle people, health and safety issues, and so on) this study has also reinforced the need for retirement community staff to be able to access training and support in a variety of areas. This would include fundamentals about how one relates to older people and ways of communicating and giving information, through to aspects such as looking at mental health needs, dealing with death and bereavement, group motivation and facilitation skills, and conflict management techniques. In addition, in other kinds of environments (for example, in specialist mental health or childcare units), management staff too would expect to have, and be given, regular support and supervision.

If an ethos of active participation and involvement is to be fully realised in these communities, then there is difficult and sensitive work to be done. It requires both frontline and managerial staff with certain attitudes and with particular skills and aptitudes. It will also involve a considerable investment of staff time at all levels beyond the instrumental, task-oriented activities of their daily jobs.

Links with the outside world

One abiding image of retirement communities, certainly from North American developments and research, is that they are self-contained developments fairly well insulated from the outside world. Sometimes, too, they are actually walled and gated communities. However, this is not the case with the research we have done in Britain. In fact, as we saw earlier, Berryhill and its residents were very keen to maintain links with the outside world in all sorts of ways, be that continuing to take part in outside activities, or having and maintaining contacts with younger generations and with families. At the same time, residents at Berryhill, like older people elsewhere (Phillipson et al, 2001), emphasised how families have their own lives to lead, and how their being resident in such an environment was important in lifting the emotional, and physical burden from families.

Aside from family relationships, Berryhill residents also wanted to retain outside connections even if contact with friends, for example, was maintained through phone calls rather than face to face. Many also desired to remain active and involved in wider community life: going to the shops, to visit their GP, and so on. Others volunteered in various ways, for instance in local schools or as ambassadors, going out to see where other retirement communities were being set up and talking to people who might be interested.

For those who both manage and staff retirement communities, the particular challenges here are to be able to articulate the kinds of links they feel are important to maintain with the outside world. To what extent should they be 'open' communities in the sense of encouraging people to come into them; and how far should they – for security reasons perhaps – be self-contained and highly security conscious? There is also a potential tension between continued family involvement and withdrawal that could be problematic unless actively addressed. As with the other issues we have discussed, much of this is about striking a balance between different needs

and expectations and finding appropriate ways of managing the inevitable tensions that will arise in retirement communities of the future.

Involving older people in research

We conclude this chapter with some brief comments about the involvement of older people in studies such as this, since this was a key feature of the participatory action research methodology we adopted. Although we did not of course conduct a parallel study of what impact the research was having, it is possible to make some observations about the mutual benefits of this approach, especially when researching new and evolving developments like a retirement community. Liz Hart and Meg Bond (1995, pp 37-8) distinguish seven criteria they regard as fundamental to an action research approach. In their view, it:

- is problem-focused, context-specific and future-oriented;
- involves change intervention;
- is a research relationship in which those involved are participants in the change process;
- is a cyclic process in which research, action and evaluation are interlinked;
- aims at improvement and involvement;
- deals with individuals as members of social groups;
- is educative.

In keeping with these points, a crucial element of our research design was to ensure that there were frequent and appropriate opportunities for residents, staff and ExtraCare themselves to be involved with the design and conduct of the study from a number of perspectives. Residents in particular contributed to our thinking about the various steps in the study through their regular inputs to the cyclical participation groups and conferencing process. They made suggestions about what questions we should and should not be asking; the design of the research instruments (notably the print size, colour and wording of the questionnaires); the ways and means of administering these instruments; how best to access difficult-to-reach groups such as family and friends; and what the most effective strategies might be for including as many residents as possible in the community conferences. They also worked with us to distribute information to their peers about the study and, on a very practical level, they put up posters, offered to hand-deliver conference invitations to all residents, and placed reminders of research events on the restaurant tables. A small number of them also took the time and trouble to keep diaries about their daily lives in Berryhill that they have subsequently shared with us.

It is our observation that many of the residents (and indeed some of the staff) became much more 'research aware' and 'research minded' over the time we worked together: they came to understand what the study was about, were able to offer insightful and pertinent comments on the findings and, in the conference discussions in particular, challenged and asked questions of the research team, of each other and of the staff who were present. At the beginning of the three years, it was quite hard to enthuse residents about the potential value of becoming involved in the study but, by the end, they could clearly articulate some of the benefits. As Alice said: "It's been an added interest as well, hasn't it?... We've had something else to look forward to, you know. It's got us together".

We would argue that, in many ways, residents' interest in the study was another manifestation of their growing self-confidence and desire to contribute constructively to discussions about the future directions for the village. A further illustration of increased research awareness was that, at the time of the first conference, there was a great deal of discussion about how Berryhill was being turned into a "nursing home" and that more and more people were being admitted who were in need of support packages and who were wheelchair dependent. Despite the presentation of figures that demonstrated that the balance between those who were on support and those who were not was about 1:2, as planned and targeted for, residents were adamant that this was changing. At the time of the second conference residents again raised this issue. We presented figures showing that the balance was still the same. In the small group discussions, residents themselves began to acknowledge that they had perhaps been wrong and that seeing someone in a wheelchair, or with an impairment, did not necessarily equate with them being on support:

> Bea: "It was right as it was when the last questionnaire was done, but I still feel that there are more people on care. That's how it appears to me. I could be totally wrong, but that's how it appears to me. When a new person comes in, the

majority of them seem to be on care when you get talking to them."

> Facilitator: "We had a not dissimilar conversation last year ... but what we are saying this time is that the results of the questionnaire don't bear that out...."

> Alice: "There's quite a lot of people on care that are quite independent and like it that way...."

> Janet: " ... people on care come down for dinner so therefore, all around the tables are wheelchairs. Able-bodied people like me that can cook for themselves – you don't see many...."

They also recognised and acknowledged that the staff were clearly managing this issue for the benefit of everyone involved:

> Petra: "Management are supposed to maintain the balance of age groups and everything in the village and it shows that that's been done properly. That's a job they were given to do, to maintain the age groups and the number of people on care, which is exactly what they've done. They're not putting more older people in. They are looking at the percentages and putting the appropriate people in to keep the population age group as they're supposed to, aren't they?"

There were some other important changes which being involved in a participatory action research project engendered. Many issues and concerns were regularly discussed and addressed as they arose (within Liaison Group meetings and through informal contacts with the management and staff) rather than necessarily waiting for 'results' at the end of a particular phase of the study. Things like helping residents and staff deal with issues around loss and bereavement were one example, with the research team putting the village in touch with an experienced bereavement counsellor. However, the most notable and concrete example of change concerns the format and conduct of street meetings, commented on here by one of ExtraCare's directors:

> "In the time that you've been doing the research, we've learnt from some of the things that you've done. The street meetings is a good example.... And we're learning better techniques to do it. Your observation about the street meetings is an

interesting one because the original assumption was that we would get a street together, and they would all share what they thought.... So, breaking that group into two, so you are now dealing with nine, is much more realistic. But, even when you've done that, then the technique of how to involve nine people is a technique that our staff need...."

Finally, although as in any study not everyone saw the relevance or importance of taking part in the research, most individuals and groups we spoke with said they were very happy to be involved and offer their views. The value of this is perhaps best encapsulated by the group interview with the management staff at Berryhill. At the end of the afternoon, they unanimously commented that never before had they had the opportunity to debate and discuss the kinds of issues we had asked them about. They had thoroughly enjoyed the interview (and had extended it by another hour!) and felt it would be valuable to have such an opportunity on a regular basis: an opportunity that would allow them some time and space together to exchange experiences and views in the midst of the constant pressures and demands on their time.

Summary and conclusion

This three-year participatory action research study of the Berryhill Retirement Village has found that:

- This community works well for its predominantly working-class population. This in turn suggests that retirement villages do not have to be planned and developed just with middle-class professional retirees in mind.
- There were clear benefits to getting involved in village life, including being able to cope better and improved self-esteem and self-confidence. However, participation in village life was sometimes affected by certain health, design and attitudinal obstacles, and varied according to individual circumstances.
- The majority of residents were highly satisfied with their flat, the village and its amenities. For women in particular, and for people who needed staff support to attend activities, the safety and security offered by having them on site was particularly valued.
- Health concerns were the prime reason for moving in. Although their health status was generally poor, substantial proportions of

respondents felt that life had got much better since moving to Berryhill, and this improvement was maintained over time.
- Keeping fit was the most important activity overall; volunteering played a large part in the life of the village; organised trips out were very popular and much appreciated; and regular street meetings offered opportunities for involvement in democratic decision making.
- Berryhill offers autonomy, security and sociability – all factors that facilitate the development of a positive environment in which to age.
- Residents reported feeling younger inside, thought they looked younger, and wanted to be younger. However, those who said they felt older than their actual age tended to have poorer physical health.
- Specific friendship groups supplied companionship and peer support in times of illness and incapacity, but for many people family remained the most important source of help and support, particularly for the women. Intergenerational links with family and friends were actively promoted and maintained, and family visited regularly.
- Future support needs were of great importance and nine out of ten people were confident that help would be available in Berryhill if they needed it. More respondents expected their physical, rather than their mental, health to worsen, and one in five were worried that their future health might affect whether the village would be a home for life.
- Family and professional helpers were supportive of Berryhill, but some external stakeholders saw the village as being exclusively for "old people"; for those who had "given up"; and as a place to move to when one could no longer cope.

In conclusion, then, in many ways this study suggests that retirement communities like Berryhill can indeed provide environments in which to age well and develop a new lifestyle in old age. They can facilitate people in their efforts to overcome illness and poor health and to enjoy a good quality of life, offering as they do a wide range of opportunities for active participation and positive ageing identities. They emphasise both the empowerment of older people, and older people as their own resource. Yet, there remain many challenges to all involved: to residents themselves whose values, attitudes and beliefs, not least around their own ageing and the ageing of others, can lead to significant tensions; to staff who may struggle to respond flexibly to the

changing needs of the individual and the community
as a whole; to developers and managers who have to
balance the benefits of increased facilities and
activities offered through greater size with the needs
of more vulnerable individuals; and, of course, to
policy makers who must judge how best to
incorporate such developments into comprehensive
strategies that promote health and well-being in
older age.

References

Age Concern (2003) 'General statistics 2002', London: Age Concern (www.ageconcern.org.uk/AgeConcern/information_426.htm).

Amarantos, E., Martinez, A. and Dwyer, J. (2001) 'Nutrition and quality of life in older adults', *Journals of Gerontology: Series A*, vol 56A, special issue II, pp 54-64.

Antonovsky, A. (1984) 'The sense of coherence as a determinant of health', in J.P. Matarazzo (ed) *Behavioural health*, New York, NY: Wiley.

Antonovsky, A. (1987) *Unravelling the mystery of health: How people manage others and stay well*, New York, NY: Wiley.

Antonovsky, A. (1996) 'The salutogenic model as a theory to guide health promotion', *Health Promotion International*, vol 11, no 1, pp 11-18.

Atkinson, P. and Hammersley, M. (1994) 'Ethnography and participant observation', in N.K. Denzin and Y.S. Lincoln (eds) *Handbook of qualitative research* (1st edn), Thousand Oaks, CA: Sage Publications, pp 248-61.

Baltes, M. and Carstensen, L. (1996) 'The process of successful ageing', *Ageing and Society*, vol 16, pp 397-422.

Baltes, P.B. and Baltes, M.M. (1993) *Successful aging: Perspectives from the behavioural sciences*, Cambridge: Press Syndicate of the University of Cambridge.

Bayley, R. (1996) *Retiring gracefully*, York: Joseph Rowntree Foundation.

Bernard, M. (2000) *Promoting health in old age*, Buckingham: Open University Press.

Bernard, M. and Phillips, J. (1998) *The social policy of old age: Moving into the 21st century*, London: Centre for Policy on Ageing.

Bernard, M., Phillips, J., Machin, L. and Harding Davies, V. (2000) *Women ageing: Changing identities, challenging myths*, London: Routledge.

Biggs, S. (1999a) *The mature imagination: Dynamics of identity in midlife and beyond*, Buckingham: Open University Press.

Biggs, S. (1999b) 'Mature imaginations: ageing and the psychodynamic tradition', *Ageing and Society*, vol 18, pp 421-39.

Biggs, S., Bernard, M., Bartlam, B. and Sim, J. (2002) 'Age, identity and anxiety within a retirement community: a new measure', Keele: Keele University (www.keele.ac.uk/depts/so/csg/age_identity.htm).

Biggs, S., Bernard, M., Kingston, P. and Nettleton, H. (1999) 'Assessing the health impact of age-specific housing', final report to the NHS Management Executive, Birmingham, West Midlands.

Biggs, S., Bernard, M., Kingston, P. and Nettleton, H. (2000) 'Lifestyles of belief: narrative and culture in a retirement community', *Ageing and Society*, vol 20, pp 649-72.

Bowling, A., Grundy, E. and Farquhar, M. (1997) *Living well into old age*, London: Age Concern.

Cameron, C. and Moss, P. (2001) *Care work: Current understandings and future directions in Europe. National report, United Kingdom*, Working Paper 3: Mapping of care services and the care workforce, London: Thomas Coram Research Unit, Institute of Education, University of London (http://144.82.35.228/carework/uk/reports/Mapping%20care.htm).

Croucher, K., Please, N. and Bevan, M. (2003) *Living at Hartrigg Oaks: Residents' views of the UK's first continuing care retirement community*, York: Joseph Rowntree Foundation.

Diener, E., Emmons, R.A., Larsen, R.J. and Griffin, S. (1985) 'The Satisfaction with Life Scale', *Journal of Personality Assessment*, vol 49, no 1, pp 71-5.

DoH (Department of Health) (2000) *Health survey for England: The health of older people*, London: DoH.

DoH (2001) *National service framework for older people*, London: DoH (www.dh.gov.uk/nsf/olderpeople).

Drewnowski, A. and Evans, W.J. (2001) 'Nutrition, physical activity, and quality of life in older adults: summary', *Journals of Gerontology: Series A*, vol 56A, special issue II, pp 89-94.

Erikson, E., Erikson, J. and Kivnick, H. (1986) *Vital involvement in old age*, New York, NY: Norton.

Erickson, M.A., Dempster-McCain, D., Whitlow, C. and Moen, P. (2000) 'Social integration and the move to a continuing care retirement community', in K. Pillemer (ed) *Social integration in the second half of life*, Baltimore, MD: The Johns Hopkins University Press, pp 211-27.

Folts, W.E. and Muir, K.B. (2002) 'Housing for older adults: new lessons from the past', *Research on Aging*, vol 24, no 1, pp 10-28.

Hart, E. and Bond, M. (1995) *Action research for health and social care: A guide to practice*, Buckingham: Open University Press.

Hochschild, H.R. (1978) *The unexpected community: Portrait of an old age subculture*, Berkeley, CA: University of California Press.

Hyde, M., Wiggins, R., Higgs, P. and Blane, D. (2003) 'A measure of quality of life in early old age: the theory, development and properties of a needs satisfaction model (CASP-19)', *Aging and Mental Health*, vol 7, no 4, pp 186-94.

Jenkinson, C., Stewart-Brown, S., Petersen, S. and Paice, C. (1999) 'Assessment of the SF-36 version 2 in the United Kingdom', *Journal of Epidemiology and Community Health*, vol 53, pp 46-50.

Jordan, K., Ong, B. and Croft, P. (2000) 'Researching limiting long-term illness', *Social Science & Medicine*, vol 50, pp 397-405.

Kastenbaum, R. (1993) 'Encrusted elders: Arizona and the political spirit of postmodern ageing', in T. Cole and A. Achenbaum (eds) *Voices and visions of ageing: Toward a critical gerontology*, New York, NY: Springer.

Kuhn, M. (1977) *Maggie Kuhn on aging*, Philadelphia, PA: Westminster.

Laws, G. (1995) 'Embodiment and emplacement', *International Journal of Aging and Human Development*, vol 40, no 4, pp 253-80.

Laws, G. (1997) 'Spatiality and age relations', in A. Jamieson, S. Harper and C. Victor (eds) *Critical approaches to ageing and later life*, Buckingham: Open University Press.

Longino, C. and McLelland, K. (1978) *Age segregation and social integration in Midwestern retirement communities*, Miami, FL: Southern Sociological Society, University of Miami.

Lucksinger, M. (1994) 'Community and the elderly', *Journal of Housing for the Elderly*, vol 11, no 1, pp 11-28.

Madigan, M.J., Mise, D.H. and Maynard, M. (1996) 'Life satisfaction and level of activity of male elderly in institutional and community settings', *Activities, Adaptation & Aging*, vol 21, no 2, pp 21-36.

Minkler, M. and Fadem, P. (2002) '"Successful aging": a disability perspective', *Journal of Disability Policy Studies*, vol 12, no 4, pp 229-35.

Moody, H. (1986) 'The meaning of life and the meaning of old age', in T. Cole and S. Gaddow (eds) *What does it mean to grow old?*, Durham, NC: Duke University Press.

Netten, A., Bebbington, A., Darton, R. and Forder, J. (2001) *Care homes for older people: Volume 1, facilities, residents and costs*, Canterbury: Personal Social Services Research Unit, University of Kent.

North Stoke Primary Care Trust (2003) *A summary of North Stoke PCT's Local Health Delivery Plan 2003/04*, Stoke-on-Trent: North Stoke Primary Care Trust.

Oberg, P. and Tornstam, L. (1999) 'Body images among men and women of different ages', *Ageing and Society*, vol 19, pp 629-44.

ODPM (Office of the Deputy Prime Minister) (2003) *Supporting people*, London: ODPM.

ONS (Office for National Statistics) (2001) *Census*, London: ONS (www.statistics.gov.uk).

Osgood, N.J. (1982) *Senior settlers: Social integration in retirement communities*, New York, NY: Praeger Publishers.

Peace, S.M. and Holland, C. (2001) *Inclusive housing in an ageing society: Innovative approaches*, Bristol: The Policy Press.

Phillips, J., Bernard, M., Biggs, S. and Kingston, P. (2001) 'Retirement communities in Britain: a "third way" for the third age?', in S.M. Peace and C. Holland (eds) *Inclusive housing in an ageing society: Innovative approaches*, Bristol: The Policy Press, pp 189-213.

Phillipson, C., Bernard, M., Phillips, J. and Ogg, J. (2001) *The family and community life of older people: social networks and social support in three urban areas*, London: Routledge.

Ray, M. (2001) 'Residents' experiences of living at the Berryhill Retirement Village: a qualitative study', final report to The ExtraCare Charitable Trust, Keele: Keele University.

Resnick, B. (2001) 'A prediction model of aerobic exercise in older adults living in a continuing-care retirement community', *Journal of Aging and Health*, vol 13, no 2, pp 287-310.

Riseborough, M. (1998) *From consumerism to citizenship: New European perspectives on independent living in older age*, London: The Housing Corporation.

Riseborough, M. (2002) 'Looking ahead to 2025. A vision for "healthy" models linking housing and care and ways people pay for it', unpublished.

Rodabough, K. (1994) 'Bofellesskab: the Danish import', in F. Edward and D. Yeatts (eds) *Housing and the ageing population: Options for the new century*, New York, NY: Garland.

Siegenthaler, K.L. and Vaughan, J. (1998) 'Older women in retirement communities: perceptions of recreation and leisure', *Leisure Sciences*, vol 20, pp 53-66.

Social Trends (2003) no 33, London: ONS (www.statistics.gov.uk/downloads/theme_social/Social_Trends33/Social_Trends_33.pdf).

Steverink, N., Westerhof, G.J., Bode, C. and Dittmann-Kohli, F. (2001) 'The personal experience of aging, individual resources, and subjective well-being', *Journal of Gerontology*, vol 56B, no 6, pp 364-73.

Streib, G.F. (2002) 'An introduction to retirement communities', *Research on Aging*, vol 24, no 1, pp 3-9.

Sumner, K. (2002) *Our homes, our lives: Choice in later life living arrangements*, London: Centre for Policy on Ageing.

Thomas, E., Wilkie, R., Peat, G., Hill, S., Dziedzic, K.S. and Croft, P.R. (2003) unpublished data from the MRC funded North Staffordshire Osteoarthritis Project, Primary Care Sciences Research Centre, Keele University.

Trinder, P. (2003) *Annual Report of the Director of Public Health: Health status profile 2002/03*, Stoke-on-Trent: North Stoke Primary Care Trust.

Tulle-Winton, E. (2000) 'Old bodies', in M. Tyler (ed) *The body, culture and society: An introduction*, Buckingham: Open University Press.

Victor, C., Scambler, S., Bond, J. and Bowling, A. (2000) 'Being alone in later life: loneliness, social isolation and living alone', *Reviews in Clinical Gerontology*, vol 10, pp 407-17.

Ware, J.E. and Sherbourne, C.D. (1992) 'The MOS 36-item Short-Form Health Survey (SF-36)', *Medical Care*, vol 30, no 6, pp 473-83.

Weisbord, M.R. and Janoff, S. (1995) *Future search: An action guide to finding common ground in organizations & communities*, San Francisco, CA: Berrett-Koehler Publishers, Inc.

Westerhof, G.J., Dittmann-Kohli, F. and Thissen, T. (2001) 'Beyond life satisfaction: lay conceptions of well-being among middle-aged and elderly adults', *Social Indicators Research*, vol 56, no 2, pp 179-203.

Appendix A:
Research questions

The study was guided by four main research questions and a series of subquestions:

1. What effect does the environment of Berryhill have on residents' well-being?
   (How does living in the village compare with previous living environments? What are the positive and negative aspects of this retirement community and how do they change over time? Does the environment facilitate or constrain the development of relationships? Does the environment enhance or impede residents' sense of well-being? Does living in Berryhill affect residents' access to support services/healthcare?)

2. What is the perceived health status of residents in Berryhill?
   (What is the perceived health status of residents? How does this vary with perceptions of (a) the physical environment; (b) the ability to manage day-to-day activities; and (c) the nature of people's relationships? How do perceptions of physical and mental health status change over time? How does this compare with population norms?)

3. How is a retirement community like Berryhill related to ageing identities and what strategies do residents adopt towards significant others?
   (How do strategies change over time? Are different strategies adopted towards different groups of significant others? How are strategies related to ageing identities? How are strategies related to involvement in the village community? What is the relationship between strategies and perceptions of health status over time? What is the relationship between strategies and sense of well-being over time?)

4. How do stakeholders view life at Berryhill?
   (How are issues of health, identity and well-being within the village viewed by families, staff, helping agencies and other community stakeholders? How do these views compare with the views of residents themselves?)

Appendix B: The study's timeline

Timeline Year One: June 2000-May 2001

	June	July	Aug	Sept	Oct	Nov	Dec	Jan	Feb	Mar	April	May
Keele Away Day (timetable for research meetings; establish Advisory Group (AG); identify current computer data; finalise research proposal; finalise research timescale)	X											
Participant observation			X						X			X
Access/introduction to Street Meetings (SMs) Access/introduction to Team Briefings Access/introduction to Management Meetings				X								
Identify diarists/set up writing support group			X						X		X	
Collection of other documentary material												
Familiarisation with documentation available: PALs, Book of Life, Minutes of meetings etc	X		X						X		X	
Draw up and circulate contact details/pen portraits of all members of AG												
Advisory Group meetings	X			X						X		
Negotiate access to pilot group Finalise pilot questionnaire to residents	X				X							
Copy pilot questionnaires (20) Pilot questionnaires							X					
Analyse results of pilot questionnaires							X					
Finalise questionnaires								X				
Print questionnaires for residents (170) Distribute questionnaires through SMs/own homes								X			X	X
Planning Conference I											X	
Preparation and submission of 1st Annual Report												X

*The timelines do not include the two-monthly liaison meetings or the weekly/fortnightly Keele team meetings.

Timeline Year Two: June 2001-May 2002

	June	July	Aug	Sept	Oct	Nov	Dec	Jan	Feb	Mar	April	May
Participant observation/diarists												
Collection of other documentary material												
Planning stakeholder interviews												
Stakeholder interviews: 1st wave												
Analysis of stakeholder interviews: 2nd wave												
Advisory Group meetings												
Planning Conference 1												
Conference 1												
Analysis of data from Conference 1												
Planning Conference 2												
Analysis of first questionnaire												
Finalise second questionnaire												
Distribute second questionnaire												
Analysis of second questionnaires												
Preparation and submission of 2nd Annual Report												

*The timelines do not include the two-monthly liaison meetings or the weekly/fortnightly Keele team meetings.

Timeline Year Three: June 2002-May 2003

	June	July	Aug	Sept	Oct	Nov	Dec	Jan	Feb	Mar	April	May
Participant observation/diarists												
Collection of other documentary material												
Collation of data from other documentary sources												
Planning stakeholder interviews: 2nd wave												
Stakeholder interviews: 2nd wave												
Analysis of stakeholder interviews: 2nd wave												
Analysis of second questionnaire												
Refine third wave questionnaire												
Distribute third questionnaire												
Analysis of data from third questionnaire												
Advisory Group meetings												
Planning Conference 2												
Conference 2												
Analysis of data from Conference 2												
Planning Conference 3												
Writing up and submission of 3rd Annual Report												

*The timelines do not include the two-monthly liaison meetings or the weekly/fortnightly Keele team meetings.

Timeline Year Four: June 2003-October 2003

	June	July	Aug	Sept	Oct
Collation of data from other documentary sources	▓	▓	▓	▓	▓
Analysis of stakeholder interviews: 3rd wave	▓	▓	▓	▓	▓
Analysis of data from third questionnaire		▓	▓	▓	
Analysis of data from Conference 3					
Planning Conference 3			▓		
Conference 3: Presentation of research findings to residents				▓	
Analysis of data from Conference 3				▓	▓
Writing up and submission of Final Report	▓	▓	▓	▓	▓

*The timelines do not include the two-monthly liaison meetings or the weekly/fortnightly Keele team meetings.

Appendix C: Questionnaires

(i) Questionnaires to residents – the tools

Short Form-12

The SF-12 is a 12-item health scale adapted from the original version SF-36 (Ware and Sherbourne, 1992). It assesses eight dimensions of health: physical functioning, mental health, social functioning, role limitations because of physical problems, role limitations because of mental problems, energy/vitality, pain and general health perceptions. For each of the items scores are calculated on a scale from 0 (worst possible health) to 100 (best possible health). Two summary scores – the physical component summary (PCS) and the mental component summary (MCS) – can be calculated. The measure has been widely adopted and used worldwide.

Diener Satisfaction with Life Scale

The SWLS is a five-item scale that measures global life satisfaction. Respondents are asked to make judgements on how satisfied or otherwise they are with their life overall. It too has been widely used in research into well-being (Diener et al, 1985). Each statement is scored from one to seven, so that the range of scores is 5 (low satisfaction) through to 35 (high satisfaction).

CASP-19

The CASP-19 is a recently developed, 19-item, quality-of-life scale. It is currently being used in the English Longitudinal Study on Ageing (Hyde et al, 2003). It is based on the theory that quality of life should be assessed on the extent to which an individual's needs are satisfied. It assesses four domains: control, autonomy, self-realisation, and pleasure. The range of scores is 0 (total absence of quality of life) through to 57 (total satisfaction on all four domains). When the study began, the CASP-19 was not available and so has been included only at Waves 2 and 3.

(ii) Questionnaires to residents – response rates

Wave 1 (2001): 159 residents/88 returns. Response rate = 55%
Wave 2 (2002): 175 residents/98 returns. Response rate = 56%
Wave 3 (2003): 169 residents/98 returns. Response rate = 58%

(iii) Questionnaires to family and friends – response rates

Eighty-three residents agreed that we could contact their relatives/friends. Of the 83 questionnaires sent, 36 were returned, a response rate of 43%.

(iv) Questionnaires to staff – response rates

Fourteen staff out of 38 returned questionnaires, a response rate of 37%.

Appendix D: Interviews

In total, 133 stakeholders were interviewed/
questionnaired:

- directors of the managing organisation: $n=3$
- developer of the village: $n=1$
- management staff at the village: $n=8$
- staff in the village: $n=1$
- GPs: $n=16$
- nurses: $n=13$
- physiotherapists: $n=4$
- occupational therapists: $n=3$
- social workers: $n=27$
- tenants in a local sheltered housing scheme (women): $n=5$
- waiting list group: $n=5$
- two groups of mixed-age residents from the two estates bordering the village: $n=5$ and $n=4$
- area housing: $n=1$
- family/friends: $n=37$

Stakeholders interview schedule

(Research questions in bold before each section of questions).

Introductions. Reminder re consent to tape. Confidentiality.

1. What is the nature of your professional contact with Berryhill?
A. **What effect does the environment of Berryhill have on residents' well-being?**

2. What sort of effects do you see the physical environment of the village as having on residents' feelings of well-being?
3. What sort of effects do you see the social environment of the village as having on residents' feelings of well-being?
B. **What is the perceived health status of residents in Berryhill?**

4. What would be your professional assessment of the physical health status of residents?
5. What would be your professional assessment of the mental health status of residents?
6. How would you see this comparing to older people in general, and in the local community?
7. How does your professional assessment of their health status compare with residents' own perceptions of their well-being in Berryhill?

C. **How is a retirement community like Berryhill related to ageing identities and what strategies do residents adopt towards significant others?**

8. How do you think residents see themselves?
9. What effect do you think living at Berryhill has on how residents see themselves?
10. How do you think you are seen by residents?
11. Compared to living in the community, how do residents maintain relationships that are important to them?

D. **How do stakeholders view life at Berryhill?**

12. Are there any general observations that you would like to make about life at Berryhill?
13. Have you seen any particular changes over time?
13a. As a group (of doctors/social workers/nurses, and so on) do you think you are doing more, or less, for people living in the village than you would be doing were they living where they did before?
14. How do you see Berryhill fitting with future service provision for older people?
14a. What are the implications of having a concentration of older people in one place?
15. If you were to sum up in one sentence what life is like at Berryhill, what would you say?

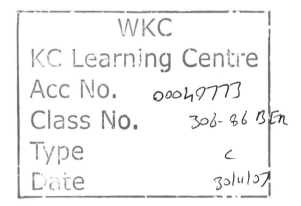

Appendix E:
Participation groups and community conferencing

Conference 1: November 2001

"Our Changing Community"

Plenary sessions: Growing Older
                         Men and Women
                         Care and Support
                         What's Life All About Then...?

Each session was followed by small group discussions, each facilitated by two members of the research team. All discussions were tape-recorded. Refreshments were available in the morning and in the afternoon, and all who attended were entered into a raffle prize draw. On average, 17 residents attended each of the four sessions. The material as presented to the residents was also given to the manager of the village for her information. A brief summary of the conference was written up for the Village newsletter, which was distributed to all residents.

Conference 2: November 2002

"Our Changing Community, A Year On: How Has Our Community Changed?"

Plenary sessions: Looking to the Future ...
                         Healthy Me
                         Current and Future Services

The same general format was adopted as for the first conference. A 10-page summary of the conference was distributed to all residents in the village, and to the management and staff teams.

Conference 3: September 2003

"Presentation of Research Findings: New Lifestyles in Old Age: Health, Identity and Well-being in Retirement Communities"

Plenary sessions: Introduction
                         Participation
                         Staying Healthy
                         Identity

All stakeholders and residents who had participated in the research were invited to attend this one-day conference.

Also available from The Policy Press